The Secrets of Early Christianity

The Dead Sea Scrolls, the Shroud of Turin, and Other Christian Mysteries

Federico Puigdvall and Francisco Javier Martinez

Cavendish Square

New York

This edition published in 2018 by Cavendish Square Publishing, LLC
243 5th Avenue, Suite 136, New York, NY 10016

First Edition

Website: cavendishsq.com

This publication represents the opinions and views of the author based on his or her personal experience, knowledge, and research. The information in this book serves as a general guide only. The author and publisher have used their best efforts in preparing this book and disclaim liability rising directly or indirectly from the use and application of this book.

All websites were available and accurate when this book was sent to press.

Cataloging-in-Publication Data

Names: Puigdevall, Federico, 1955-. | Martínez, Francisco Javier.
Title: The secrets of early Christianity / Federico Puigdevall and Francisco Javier Martínez.
Description: New York : Cavendish Square Publishing, 2018. | Series: The secrets of history | Includes bibliographical references and index.
Identifiers: ISBN 9781502632739 (library bound) | ISBN 9781502634412 (pbk.)
Subjects: LCSH: Christianity--Juvenile literature. | History--Religious aspects--Christianity--Juvenile literature. | Church history--Juvenile literature.
Classification: LCC BR125.5 P85 2018 | DDC 230--dc23

Editorial Director: David McNamara
Editor: Erica Grove
Associate Art Director: Amy Greenan
Production Coordinator: Karol Szymczuk

Original Idea: Sol90 Publishing
Project Management: Nuria Cicero
Editorial Coordination: Diana Malizia
Editorial Team: Alberto Hernández, Virginia Iris Fernández, Mar Valls, Marta de la Serna, Sebastián Romeu. Maximiliano Ludueña, Carlos Bodyadjan, Doris Elsa Bustamante, Tania Domenicucci, Andrea Giacobone, Constanza Guariglia, Joaquín Hidalgo, Hernán López Winne.
Proofreaders: Marta Kordon, Edgardo D'Elio
Design: Fabián Cassan
Layout: Laura Ocampo, Carolina Berdiñas, Clara Miralles, Paola Fornasaro, Mariana Marx, Pablo Alarcón

The photographs in this book are used by permission and through the courtesy of: Corbis Images; Getty Images; National Geographic Stock; Topfoto, Granger, Other Images; Alamy; HolyLAndPhotos (www.HolyLandPhotos.org); John M. Allegro, Allegro Estate; Israel Antiquities Authority, Clara Amit; Photos © The Israel Museum, Jerusalem; AGE Fotostock; L. Garlaschelli; Barry M. Schwortz Collection, STERA Inc.; Petaqui; Kris Simoens; Sacred Destinations Images; Dr. Leen Ritmeyer; Mitchell Library, State Library of New South Wales.

Printed in the United States of America

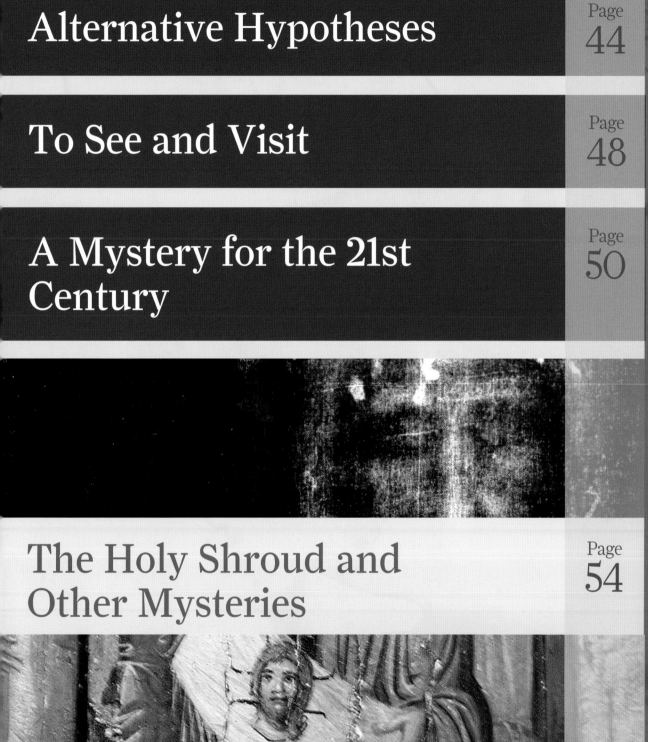

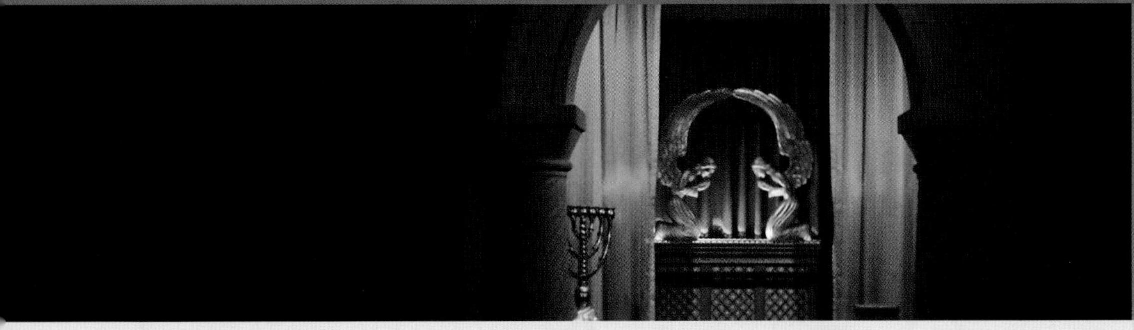

An Invaluable Source for Monotheism

In 1947, before the dust had settled from the Second World War, the academic world was shaken by news that was transmitted nearly in secret: in the area around the Dead Sea, some manuscripts had been discovered that contained religious messages recorded by the Essenes, a Judaic sect about which very little was known. While searching for a lost goat, a young Bedouin named Muhammed edh Dhib saw a small opening in the hillside, peeked into the entrance, and found some jars piled inside the cave. They contained several very ancient manuscripts, which he brought to a merchant in Bethlehem named Kando, who paid him a few dollars for the find. This event sparked a frenetic search to find more scrolls. News of the discovery came to the attention of a Catholic Priest named Roland de Vaux, who was the director of the L'École Biblique et archéologique française de Jerusalén, and he began to search for manuscripts on his own.

The first three scrolls were purchased from Kando, the astute Bethlehem merchant, by Eliezer Sukenik, a professor from the Hebrew University of Jerusalem. The first translations were made and published and their contents shocked both historians and theologians. Not surprising, since they involved the most significant finding in the field of monotheism. The texts appeared to refer to Christianity, but that was impossible, as they were dated from a period before its existence. It was determined that they were from the Judaic sect called the Essenes, who are not even mentioned in the New Testament, which turned the finding into an enigma. All that was known was that the historian Flavius Josephus had dedicated more pages to the Essenes than to any other Judaic sect of the first century. It was suspected that their omission from the New Testament had been meant to eliminate what would be the main link that bound Judaism to the nascent Christianity.

When they learned that the scrolls described a leader called "Teacher of Righteousness," the theologians paled, as it seemed a portrait of Jesus. They also spoke of two Messiahs: one princely, from the line of David, and the other priestly, from the line of Aaron or Zadok. At first glance, it appeared to speak of Jesus and His cousin, John the Baptist. Heated arguments were unleashed both for and against this assumption. The discovery of the Dead Sea Scrolls and their delayed translation is a unique scenario that involves intrigue, robberies, violence, an oral trial, and other elements that have become the "academic scandal of the twentieth century," in the opinion of historian Geza Vermes. There are many manuscripts of unknown origin (possibly in the hands of collectors who purchased them on the antiquities black market). Is it possible that Jesus and John the Baptist were Essenes? Were they pacifists, or did they call for violence against the Romans? Would the Temple Scroll have been a sixth biblical text that would have turned the Pentateuch into a Hexateuch? Can the sudden enrichment of the Knights Templar of the twelfth century be attributed to having found some of the treasures mentioned in the Copper Scroll? Would the marriage of Mary and Joseph have been a "dynastic marriage," as mentioned in the Community Rule Manuscript? Why are the Essenes not mentioned in the New Testament? Are there more manuscripts that we still don't know about, in the Vatican or some other obscure location? The list of questions generated is immense and presents an enigma that merits a productive debate about true Biblical history. The reader will have to decide which of the hypotheses developed on the following pages appear most valid.

Jorge Dulitzky

Argentine historian and Egyptologist, specialist in Biblical history. He is the author of the books *Akenatón, el faraón olvidado* (*Akhenaten, the Forgotten Pharaoh*) (2004) and *Los rollos del Mar Muerto y las raíces secretas del cristianismo* (*The Dead Sea Scrolls and the Secret Roots of Christianity*) (2007).

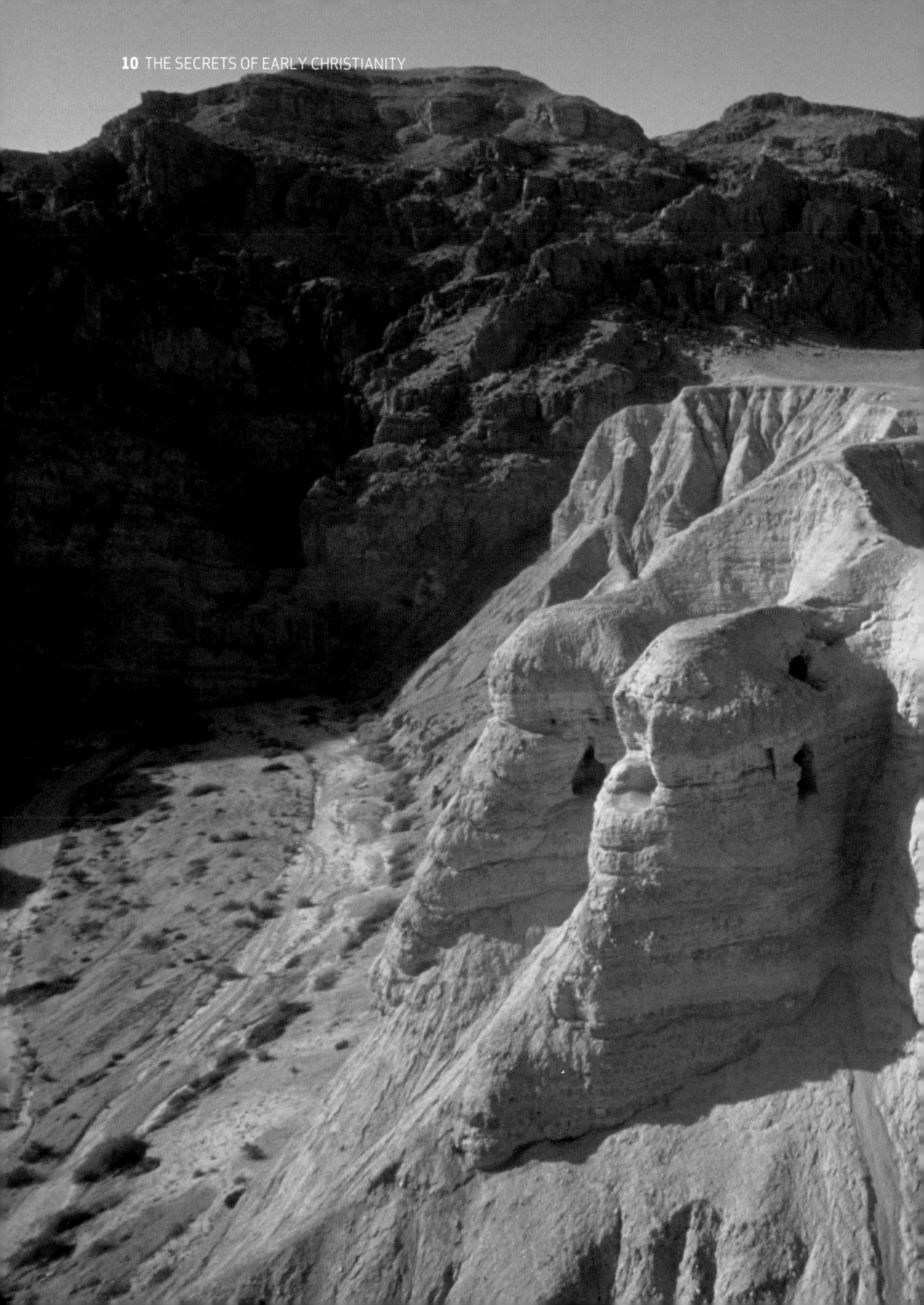

SECRET IN THE CAVES
You can see the various entrances into the caves of Qumran, where the valuable Biblical manuscripts were found.

Secret Writings of the Dead Sea

Their discovery has shed new light on Judaism and early Christianity, but since their finding was publicized in 1947, they have been the subject of great controversy. Who wrote them? What secrets do they still hold?

Between November and December of 1946, a Bedouin shepherd of the Ta'amirah tribe tending a herd of goats near a place called Khirbet Qumran ("Qumran ruins" in Arabic), in a valley in the desert of Judea some 1.24 miles (two kilometers) from the western coasts of the Dead Sea, decided to climb a steep incline up one of the cliff walls to rescue some of his animals which had moved away from the rest of the herd. That was how Muhammed edh Dhib came to enter a cave, one among a large number of caverns in the region excavated as of long ago, and about which there were all manner of legends. His curiosity was aroused when after throwing a stone inside the cave, a sound came back through the darkness that seemed to be that of a jug breaking. He imagined he had found a treasure, but it was already late in the day, and he left the cave. He returned to the place the next day, together with his cousins Yuma Muhammed and Jalil Musa, to explore it more fully. They found the floor of the cave covered with pieces of ceramic, and along a cave wall they found several narrow jars that appeared to be buried, some of which still retained an ancient seal.

DIFFERENT TREASURE

They opened and examined the insides of the jugs, but they did not find jewels or gold. The receptacles contained only old parchments, some of them tied with rags, with writings in a language they couldn't understand. It is said that they used one of them to make a fire to keep warm, and in the end they decided to take several of them to offer to a local merchant. The parchments were hung for some time on a post in a Bedouin shop, until they were sold to an antiquarian in Bethlehem, Ibrahim Iya, who in turn contacted a professional seller, Faidi al-Alami. The latter, suspecting that the merchandise might be stolen, refused to deal with it, so Yuma Muhammed, the Bedouin, went to an Orthodox Christian Syrian, George Ishaya, also known as George Isaias. Isaias knew the perfect man to make the sale: Jalil, also known as Kando, a cobbler in Bethlehem, who placed the manuscripts in the hands of the young Syrian Orthodox bishop of the Monastery of Saint Mark in Jerusalem, Anastasio Yeshue Samuel.

BIBLICAL SCROLL
The long parchment with the *Book of Isaiah*, in a photo from 2008. This manuscript was the first one found, in cave one, and is the one in the best condition.

Bishop Samuel, an astute man, thought the scrolls were older than the scholars with whom he had consulted stated, and continued to search for someone to adequately evaluate the scrolls. This made their discoverers think that a real treasure was definitely hidden in the cave in Qumran where these had been found. So they set off again, this time accompanied by the Syrian Isaias, and they found more jars and scrolls. This time Faidi al-Alami purchased three scrolls for seven pounds sterling, and in turn went to one of his partners in Jerusalem, the Armenian Christian Nasri Ohan. It was the latter who brought them to a professor at the Hebrew University of Jerusalem, Eleazar Sukenik, a noted expert in ancient Hebrew epitaphs, and who immediately advised Nasri Ohan that the scrolls were authentic and certainly very ancient. This took place on November 25, 1947. Four days later, on November 29 of that year (the precise day on which the General Assembly of the United Nations voted in favor of the division of Palestine into two states, and the establishment of the State of Israel), Nasri Ohan and Eleazar Sukenik traveled to Bethlehem and returned with two more scrolls. Sukenik, not having much money, but having a lot of time and patience, would manage, with great effort, to acquire more

manuscripts during the subsequent months. Meanwhile, Samuel the bishop had not been able to find anyone who believed in the authenticity of his scrolls until, in January of 1948, he contacted Sukenik, who, after examining them, concluded that they were the most valuable Biblical manuscripts discovered to date. The intrigue of this fascinating archeological discovery was reaching its climax, and doing so at a troubled time in the history of Israel and therefore, of all the Middle East. In 1948, the British mandate for

Palestine was finalized, and the war between the Arabs and the Israelis began—the first of the bloody chapters that were later known as the Arab-Israeli Conflict, which still lingers and which in fact began the very day after the UN's recognition of the State of Israel. The conflict lasted more than a year, with Lebanese, Syrian, Iraqi, Egyptian, and Transjordanian troops participating, supported by Libyan, Saudi, and Yemeni volunteers, who came together for the defense of the Arab territories in

CAVE 4
Interior of Cave 4, where most of the fragments were found. It is actually two interconnected artificial caves. The cave was discovered in September of 1952.

SAMARITANS
This image from the 1940s shows Samaritan priests with the Samaritan Torah. Their religion is closely related to Judaism. Some 5% of the writings from Qumran are from this tradition.

the recently proclaimed Jewish State. It ended with the armistice of 1949, and with Israel's victory, which expanded the territory that had been grated by the 1947 partition plan by more than 1,931 mi² (5,000 km²).

OTHER FINDINGS IN QUMRAN
In this confrontational environment, bishop Samuel had been "advised" not to deal with the Israelis. Therefore, being determined to study the manuscripts, he went to the Americans, who directed him to the organization American Schools of Oriental Research

(ASOR), in Jerusalem. There, the first photographs of the bishop's scrolls were taken: the text of *Isaiah*, the so-called *Community Rule and the Pesher Habakkuk* (the word *pesher* is derived from the Hebrew for "interpret," and is frequently used to introduce the explanation of a fragment of the Scriptures). A short time later, on April 11, 1948, the first report on the manuscripts would be written, through the central offices of the American Schools of Oriental Research, in New Haven. All of the important newspapers in the

United States and Europe echoed the news immediately: original copies of the Hebrew Bible, much older than any previously known of, had been discovered. The news spread like wildfire and brought about numerous confrontations and conflicts: between the scholars, regarding access to the scrolls and to the first publications; between archeologists and Bedouins, who fought in the search for new caves and manuscripts; between the States of Israel and Jordan for control of the Qumran area; and between the

Judaic and Christian experts, who tirelessly debated about the interpretation and ultimate meaning of the valuable writings that had been found. In this context, William Foxworth Albright (1891–1971), the director of ASOR, archeologist, linguist, and ceramics expert, is credited with confirming the authenticity of the parchments and announcing that they pertained to the period between 250 BCE and 100 CE.
These parchments, which would later become known as the "Dead Sea Manuscripts

Continued on page 18 ▶

Qumran Caves

There are a total of 11 caves. Manuscripts have been found on papyrus and parchment (as well as one copper scroll) in various states of preservation. Many of the writings are Biblical (canonical or apocryphal) and others are specific to the religious community that copied the texts.

The manuscripts

The Dead Sea scrolls are one of the most important discoveries of modern times. They were found between 1947 and 1956 along the Northeast coast of the Dead Sea. They include nearly 900 texts written on more than 15,000 fragments. Most of them are written on parchment in coal-based ink.

The archeological sites

Besides the 11 Caves of Qumran, other scrolls were found at nearby sites between 1951 and 1963. These explorations were motivated by the discovery of the Dead Sea scrolls. These scrolls are also included under the general title of the Dead Sea manuscripts.

Qumran Valley

Many manuscripts hidden in caves, some rolled inside vessels, were found in the Desert of Judea, in the region of Qumran. Most of the texts are written in Hebrew, Aramaic, and some in Greek.

Qumran ruins

These were known before the scrolls were discovered. From the beginning, the ruins have been related to the manuscripts.

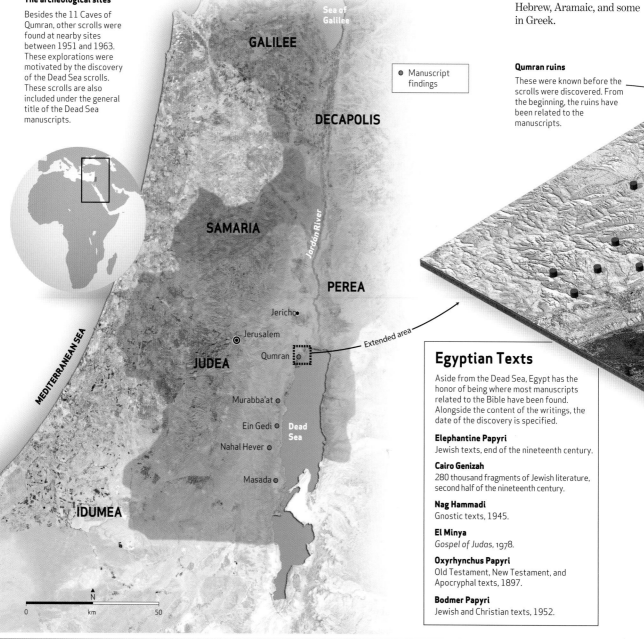

● Manuscript findings

MEDITERRANEAN SEA

Sea of Galilee

GALILEE

DECAPOLIS

SAMARIA

Jordán River

PEREA

Jericho

Jerusalem

Qumran — Extended area

JUDEA

Murabba'at

Ein Gedi — Dead Sea

Nahal Hever

Masada

IDUMEA

Cav

N
0 — km — 50

Egyptian Texts

Aside from the Dead Sea, Egypt has the honor of being where most manuscripts related to the Bible have been found. Alongside the content of the writings, the date of the discovery is specified.

Elephantine Papyri
Jewish texts, end of the nineteenth century.

Cairo Genizah
280 thousand fragments of Jewish literature, second half of the nineteenth century.

Nag Hammadi
Gnostic texts, 1945.

El Minya
Gospel of Judas, 1978.

Oxyrhynchus Papyri
Old Testament, New Testament, and Apocryphal texts, 1897.

Bodmer Papyri
Jewish and Christian texts, 1952.

Why is the Book of Esther not among the manuscripts found in the caves?

There are several copies of the other books in the Hebrew Bible. There are many possible explanations. On one side there is evidence that this book was created among "gentiles" (Babylonian or Persian). On another side, even though the text is important as a reaffirmation of the Jewish identity, it has little religious value; in fact, the name of God is never mentioned in it. It is believed that this is one of the last books to be included in the Bible.

enigmas

Caves with pottery pieces

In addition to the caves with the manuscripts, many other caves were found that contained pieces of broken pottery similar to the ones that served to protect the scrolls.

Judea Desert

Cave 11

Cave 3

Cave 1

Cave 2

Parchment and papyrus

80% of the writings are on scrolls made mostly of goat or sheep skins, and some are also made from gazelle or ibex skins. The rest are papyrus, made of plant material (only in Cave 7) and there is one copper scroll (in Cave 3).

Cave 4

Cave 5

Cave 7

Cave 8

Cave 9

Cave 10

JUDEA

DEAD SEA

Caves with manuscripts

The caves were given a number following the order of their discovery. Numbers 1 and 11 are the ones with the best quality manuscripts. Cave 4 was the cave with most fragments found.

(or Scrolls)," were indeed the most ancient of their kind ever found. Before that, the oldest Hebrew manuscripts of the Tanakh (or Hebrew Bible) were two medieval codices, from the years 920 and 1008 (the Aleppo Codex and the Leningrad Codex, respectively). These newly discovered writings had proceeded the oldest known copies of Hebrew Scriptures by more than a thousand years. The Nash Papyrus (2nd Century BCE) had been discovered, but contained only 24 lines. The finding caused fervent searches in the Qumran area, a narrow and arid plot of land near the Ayin Feshja oasis, 1,230 feet (375 meters) below sea level. Between 1950 and 1960, hundreds of caves in the area were explored. Ten of them (in addition to the original) also contained writings. The territory (like other caves in areas surrounding Qumran) is within the West Bank, which was part of Jordan until 1967. That year, Israel conquered the West Bank during the Six-Day War. Today, nearly all of the manuscripts are in Israel and under its control. Archeologists found a multitude of fragments (very few manuscripts have remained intact through the years), and in all, 900 writings in ancient Hebrew, Aramaic, Nabatean, and Greek have been restored. Within these appear fragments of all the books of the Old Testament with the exception of the Book of Esther, as well as writings related to history and the mysterious laws of the Judaic community that inhabited the locale. There are also "apocryphal" books—that is, books that were not later included in the canon of the Hebrew Bible. Is it possible that the writers and final guardians of the manuscripts were the Essenes, a Judaic community of which some scholars state John the Baptist was a member, as well as Jesus, according to the most daring? These questions remain controversial to this day. The investigators next established a classification system for the wri-

tings. They are assigned first the number given to each cave, then a Q (for Qumran), and next a number or initial referring to the fragment in question. So, for example, the first would be 1Q1, and the last 11Q23. Cave 4 has proven to be the most fruitful: discovered in 1952, it was really two interconnected caves, and contained 90% of the manuscripts and fragments found altogether. However, some of the more controversial scrolls were not found in Cave 4. It has been postulated that manuscript 7Q5 is none other than part of the Gospel of Mark, a controversial thesis that has caused sharp confrontations between many scholars, since the scientific consensus is that there were no New Testament writings in the caves of Qumran.

DELICATE NEGOTIATIONS

Not only papyrus and manuscripts were found in the caves. Beginning in 1951, teams led by Gerald Lankester Harding (Director of the Jordanian Department of Antiquities of the John Rockefeller Museum) and Roland de Vaux (from the Ècole Biblique et archéologique française de Jérusalem, editors of the famous Jerusalem Bible), both established in eastern Jerusalem, took charge of the excavations in the area south of Qumran. Evidence was found that the caves had been used since the Copper Age (c. 4000 BCE). In the cavities explored in the Nahal Darga, a cleft known by the Arab name of Wadi Al-Murabba'at, they found Arabic coins, objects and writings from the seventh and fourteenth centuries CE. Pieces of ceramic and sacred scarabs from the middle Bronze Age (c. 2000 BCE) were also found, as well as an administrative papyrus drafted in Paleo-Hebrew that can be dated to the late Iron Age (c. 650 BCE), the period of the last kings of Judah. This papyrus is written in the same ancient Hebrew that was preserved many centuries later in some scrolls from Qumran to write the sacred name of God

William F. Albright
1891–1971

Born in Chile, son of an evangelical pastor, he received his doctorate from Johns Hopkins University in Baltimore (U.S.). During the first half of the twentieth century, he was considered the highest authority on Biblical matters; in fact, Albright was the first to validate the authenticity of the Dead Sea manuscripts (in 1948), after examining the first photographs taken of them. Albright was twice the director of the American Schools of Oriental Research (ASOR) in Jerusalem, and conducted numerous excavations in Palestine. He founded the Biblical Archeology School, which had strong influence on studies of the historical aspects of the Bible.

EMINENCE Albright determined the legitimacy of the Dead Sea Scrolls. His archeological endeavors brought about a new way of addressing Biblical studies.

Hershel Shanks
1930

American author specializing in Biblical archeology. Founder of the Biblical Archeology Society and editor of the bimonthly publication *Biblical Archeology Review*. In 1991, he edited a volume of copies of the Dead Sea Scrolls, thus ending the monopoly of a small academic group over the writings.

CONTROVERSY His publications caused controversy, but allowed more people to study the scrolls.

◀ *From page 15*   *Continued on page 22* ▶

Roland de Vaux
1903–1971

French priest, archeologist, and historian, born in Paris. He entered the Dominican order of the priesthood in 1929. In 1934, he emigrated to Jerusalem, where he remained until his death. There, he worked at the prestigious École Biblique, eventually becoming director. In 1949, the director of the Jordanian Department of Antiquities, the British Gerald Lankester Harding, recruited him to search for new scrolls, after the first manuscript findings in the caves of Qumran. Beginning in 1951, he led the excavations in the archeological site in Qumran. De Vaux became head of the team exclusively studying the manuscripts. His team included the Hungarian Jozef Milik, the Frenchman Pierre Benoit and the British John M. Allegro and John Strugnell. First

Benoit, and later Strugnell, headed the manuscript translation teams after the death of de Vaux. Beginning with his studies in the Qumran ruins and nearby caves, de Vaux affirmed that both sites were related, that Qumran had been inhabited by a community of Essenes, and that the place had later been destroyed by the Romans in the year 68 CE, during the First Jewish-Roman War. He wrote *The Institutions of the Old Testament* (1960) and *Archeology and the Dead Sea Manuscripts* (1962).

THE LEADER De Vaux controlled, almost from the beginning, the numerous fragments of the manuscripts, as well as the on-site excavations in Qumran.

"All the discoveries in Qumran are compatible with what the manuscripts tell us about the community."

Emanuel Tov
1941

Born in Amsterdam, Netherlands, he emigrated to Israel in 1961. He studied at the Hebrew University of Jerusalem, where he has been a professor since 1986. In 1990, he became editor-in-chief of the official project for publication of the Dead Sea manuscripts by the Oxford Press.

Under his direction, they appeared in 33 volumes between 1992 and 2009. In 1989, he wrote *Textual Criticism of the Hebrew Bible*, which enjoyed great critical and popular success. In 2009, the State of Israel awarded him the Israel Prize in Biblical Research.

EDITOR Emanuel Tov was able to facilitate the process of publication of the manuscripts, once their study had been opened to people outside of the initial select group of specialists.

The Ruins of Qumran

Known as Khirbet Qumran, the ruins were explored between 1951 and 1956 with the aim of finding a link between the writings in the caves and the adjacent ruins. The city was occupied by the Roman Empire and the archeological remains point to a violent ending.

The Citadel

It is about a mile from the Western coast of the Dead Sea, on top of a cliff. The walls were destroyed by the Romans. A layer of ashes covers the citadel area where many arrowheads were found.

Inkwell

This bronze inkwell supports the hypothesis that Qumran was a site where copies of texts were made.

AQUEDUCT

It takes water from the Wadi Qumran stream.

N
O   E
S

83 m

50 m

95 m

90 m

CAVE 4

The closest cave to the ruins.

CIUDADELA

CEMETERY

It contains around 1,200 aligned individual tombs. Most belong to men and only 100 belong to women and children.

Kitchen

Tower

Vessels

The vessels found in the ruins are identical to the ones that contained the scrolls in the caves.

Courtyard

Aqueduct entrance

Defensive structure

The lack of external walls and the easy access indicate that the inhabitants did not expect imminent attacks, but the tower and the side walls suggest a defensive approach.

Water and the cisterns

The building with various tanks permits water storage. It is believed that it was used for drinking as well as for baths and pottery works.

Aqueduct

enigmas

What was the war of the Sons of Light against the Sons of Darkness about?

One of the most mysterious documents found in the caves is the one known as: "The war of the Sons of Light against the Sons of Darkness" or the "War Manuscript." This is a military strategy manual that describes an apocalyptic war between these two groups. The community that wrote it called themselves the Sons of Light, while the Sons of Darkness were the enemies that can be identified with the Romans or with other Jewish groups considered to be corrupt.

The *scriptorium*

One of the central rooms in the everyday life of the settlement, it is believed that the papyrus scrolls and parchments were written and stored here.

14 m

4.5 m

Pottery workshop

Water cistern

Refectory and meeting room
The spaciousness of this room allowed for collective community activities to be held there.

Storeroom

Water cistern

Stables

THE RUINS TODAY

With topography characteristic of the Qumran desert, the site's ruins are located on a terrace of clay loam and sand that is easy to dig into (many of the caves are man-made). The whole area including the ruins and the caves are part of an Israeli National Park.

A society divided

During the first century CE, at the end of the Second Temple period (at the dawn of Christianity), the Jewish people were divided into various factions that disagreed on matters of religious interpretation, as well as the way of addressing their difficult relationship with the political authorities (Rome had conquered Judea in 63 BCE). Although majority opinion continues to identify the Essenes as the guardians of the Dead Sea manuscripts, different scholars have described the community that preserved these writings as one of the parties that made up the Jewish society of the era. The two main groups were the Pharisees on one hand, and the Sadducees on the other. Then, and in significantly lower numbers, came the Essenes. Flavius Josephus (and later Philo of Alexandria), calculated their number at some four thousand people. Lastly,

an additional group—very scarce in numbers—was the zealots ("Zealous" in their devotion to God). This group carried Jewish law to limits considered extreme by other Jews, and sought freedom from the Roman yoke at all costs. An extreme faction of this group were the Sicari, who went so far as to murder other Jews who did not cooperate with their plans for rebellion against Rome. A group

of Zealots became the last bastion of resistance during the Great Jewish Revolt (or First Jewish-Roman War), taking the fort of Masada in 66 CE. Masada fell to the Romans in 73 CE (three years after Jerusalem, and five years after Qumran). When the Romans got through the walls, they found that all of its occupants had committed suicide.

ISOLATED FORTRESS
Masada was the last site of resistance to the Roman siege during the Great Jewish Revolt. Manuscripts were found inside its ruins.

Too many dishes

More than a thousand pieces of dishware (plates, bowls, cups) were found in one small room in Qumran. To Roland de Vaux, it was an indication of the importance of communal food in the group (they ate together, but each with their own individual plate). Others thought differently—that Qumran could have been a commercial center where ceramics were produced. The plates would have been merchandise for sale. Still others thought that Qumran could have been an inn for travelers and merchants, and the dishware was meant to provide for the demands of visitors.

PROFUSION OF PLATES
The large number of receptacles in Qumran has given rise to different explanatory hypotheses.

(YHWH), as a sign that it should not be pronounced. The vast collection of religious and theological works found in these places was written largely during the three centuries before the destruction of the temple in Jerusalem by the Romans in the year 70 CE, which gave rise to the Great Jewish Revolt (or First Jewish-Roman War).

◀ From page 18

WELL-KEPT SECRETS

The guardians of the scrolls, before the Romans destroyed Qumran around 68 CE, wrapped papyri and parchments in several layers of cloth, stored them inside clay jars sealed with some type of hermetic seal, and hid them in caves to preserve them from destruction. Since their discovery, there have been all types of conjecture about the final intentions of their writers and compilers, but one fact is indisputable: the writings were extremely important to the people who wrote them, copied them, and hid them, and they made up a great library that was commonly and frequently used among the inhabitants of Qumran. Through their care of the manuscripts, they ensured that the writings (with some help from the dry, arid climate of the region) would provide us with a marvelous legacy, an authentic treasure for the culture of humanity. A treasure that, for all the efforts of the researchers and scholars, continues to keep its secrets.

DEAD SEA
Salt banks on the shores of the Dead Sea. Along its western coast, various Jewish archeological sites were found with antique manuscripts of immense historical value.

The Qumran Complex

The caves in which the manuscripts were found are just a few meters from the ruins of Qumran, which would appear to suggest an undeniable link between the two sites. The identity of their occupants is still subject to debate. A few meters to the east of this settlement is a cemetery, which belonged to the ancient community.

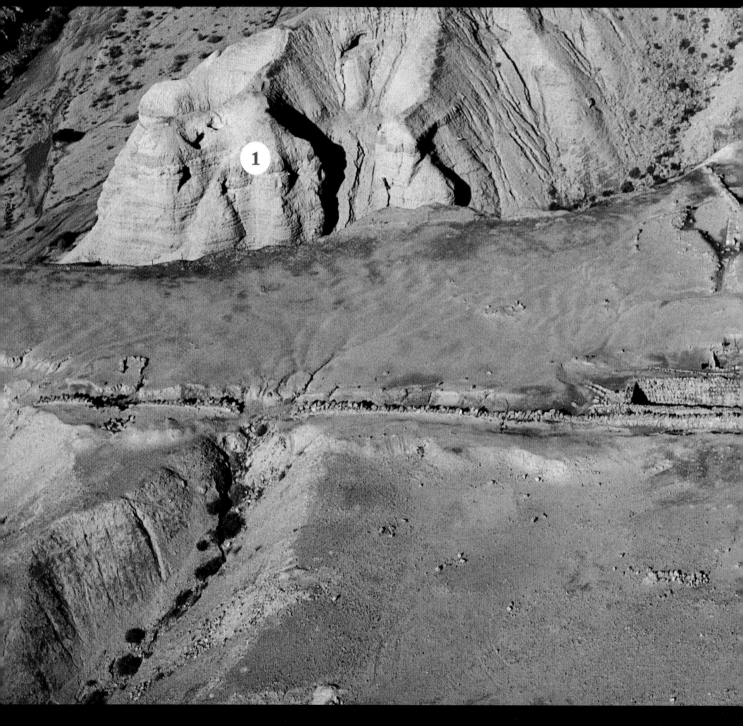

 STOREHOUSE OF WRITINGS
There is evidence that humans have been using these caves for six thousand years. In the third

to have used a scroll stored in a vase from a cave close to Jericho when editing the Old

 COMMUNITY CENTER
The settlement was populated by a celibate community although,

Cisterns

A dozen cisterns have been found in Qumran, which for the most part are accessed by steps. The features of these tanks have given rise to different theories regarding the purpose of Qumran, other than the most commonly supported theory that it served as a monastic refuge. It has also been suggested that it served as a Jewish fortress, a business center, a factory, and a library.

2

3

4, married couples were allowed to live in Qumran, provided they maintained a life of celibacy after joining the movement.

 THE CEMETERY
Adjacent to the citadel (114.8 ft [35 m] to the east) there is a cemetery, which was where the first archeological digs took place in 1855. The tombs have been a source of controversy and contradictory suggestions regarding their origin.

Who Wrote the Scrolls?

They lived in the desert, possessed no personal goods, spent their days studying the Law, and observed a strict code of conduct. They preserved the Qumran scrolls, but who were they?

The Essenes were a Jewish community that inhabited the area surrounding the Dead Sea, south of Jericho and north of Ein Gedi. At the midway point between these two sites, the ruins of Qumran are found. The Essenes, whose origins may date back to an adoptive son of Moses, from whom they took their name, considered that they had been chosen by God to lead the fight against "the Sons of Darkness." There is no mention of them in the New Testament. This Jewish religious group, well documented by Romano-Jewish historian Flavius Josephus, flourished between the second century BCE and the first century CE. The group was ascetic in practice and eschatological in their interpretation of contemporary history. Although their presence was somewhat smaller than the Pharisees and Sadducees, the two main groups into which Judaism was divided at the time, the Essenes were relatively important in some towns and villages, mainly in Judea. It is believed that they inhabited the ruins at Qumran and were the guardians of the Dead Sea Scrolls, of which it is believed they were authors, partly as scribes and partly as simple preservers.

OTHER THEORIES

However, there are other scholars that believe that the Essenes themselves were not responsible for the Qumran movement, attributing credit to a group that broke away from the main movement in the second century BCE. The Essenes were a closely integrated and very well-organized community, although there were some independent branches of the structure, some of which abided by a strict rule of celibacy. Its members, having been educated and having spent a two-year test period before being definitively welcomed into the community (supposedly into a desert retreat), took an oath, relinquished all their possessions, and dedicated their lives to studying the Torah. They were obliged to always tell the truth, they practiced humility, and strictly observed a rigorous code of conduct built on brotherhood. Like other communities during that period, they were self-sufficient thanks to agriculture. The fruits of their personal labors (they participated in certain trades that were useful to the community), were distributed based on the needs of each member, although they always set aside a portion to assist the

enigmas

What Purpose Did the Qumran Cisterns Serve?

The excavation work carried out by Roland de Vaux unearthed dozens of cisterns at Qumran. The steps that descended to the bottom of the cisterns could suggest that they were bathing pools used in purification rituals; this was the conclusion reached by de Vaux. However, other researchers believe that the water that reached the cisterns was impure and could not have been employed for such rituals. Archeologists Yitzhak Magen and Yuval Peleg believe that Qumran was a ceramics factory. The cisterns may have been used to produce clay with which the ceramics typical of Qumran may have been made. During a 2004 excavation, 12 inches (30 centimeters) of pure clay were found at the bottom of a cistern. Below is an example of an iron and bronze ritual pot.

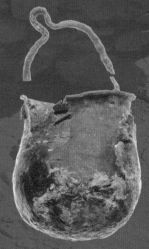

COMMUNITY ROOM Ruins identified by Roland de Vaux as the Qumran refectory.

Turbulent Times

The period during which the scrolls were written (third century BCE to first century CE) was an especially turbulent time for the Jewish community. After the destruction of the First Temple (built by Solomon in 957 BCE) by Babylon in 587 BCE and the resulting slavery of the Jews, Judea came under the rule of the Persian Empire (539 BCE). In 516 BCE, work on the Second Temple was completed. Some time later, control of Jerusalem passed to the Seleucid Empire (the dynasty that succeeded Alexander the Great, who had vanquished the Persians in 333 BCE). The Maccabean Revolt that took place in 167 BCE resulted in Jewish independence, establishing the Hasmonean dynasty, which lasted until 63 BCE, when the region was conquered by Rome. In 66 CE, the First Jewish–Roman War (or The Great Revolt) broke out, ending four years later with the total defeat of the Jews and the destruction of the Second Temple (and the beginning of the diaspora), by the future Roman Emperor Titus.

most unfortunate or outsiders that needed their help. Qumran may have been inhabited since ancient times. It is believed that the area was first settled at the end of the First Temple period (eighth to seventh century BCE), as the ruins of an old fortress from the Kingdom of Judah have been excavated, believed by some to be Seccacah, one of the six desert lands of the Ancient Kingdom of Israel. Another settlement was established on the site around the second century BCE, during the reign of John Hyrcanus (135–104 BCE), with the existing structure restored and expanded during the first century BCE. The settlement may have been destroyed by the earthquake and the resulting fire in 31 BCE; however, it would appear that it was rebuilt by those who inhabited the area during the reign of the ethnarch Herod Archelaus (4 BCE to 6 CE) son of Herod the Great and brother of Herod Antipas. In all likelihood, Qumran was a spiritual center in which only a dozen community leaders lived on a permanent basis, with said leaders assuming responsibility for preserving the sacred texts. Around 200 people lived in the surrounding tents and caves. In addition to upholding the Law (the Torah), they believed it was their duty to preserve the scrolls which contained the Word of God, and it is possible that they gathered together several thousand texts, which would have come to represent one of the period's oldest and most interesting libraries. While the creation of all the writings held in the library cannot be attributed exclusively to the Essenes, as it has been demonstrated that several of the scrolls are much older and some came from a number of difference sources, it is evident that the community played a role in preserving and studying the texts.

ENIGMATIC ROOM
The discovery of a large room in the main building at Qumran in which, in addition to remnants of benches and low tables made of mud

Qumran Inkwells

At the ruins of Qumran, in a room called the *scriptorium*, which it is believed was used to make copies of the scrolls, a number of inkwells were found. Two of them (below) were ceramic, modest in appearance and Roman in style. Another type of inkwell was much more elaborate, larger in size size at 3 inches (8 centimeters) in height, compared to the ceramic inkwells which measured 2 inches (6 centimeters) and made of bronze. Although these implements are one of the main reasons for linking Qumran to the scrolls found in the caves, no evidence of parchments has been found in the ruins. The ink used on the scrolls was mainly black, although in some cases a bluish ink was used and, in very scarce instances, the ink was red in color. Examinations have shown that a coal-based ink was used. This type of ink was found in the bronze inkwell.

PLUNDERING THE TEMPLE
The Arch of Titus in Rome recalls the victory over the Jews and the plundering of treasure found in the Second Temple in Jerusalem.

A COPY CENTER?
Evidence seems to suggest that at least some of the scrolls were copied (or composed) at the ruins of Qumran.

Flavius Josephus

Josephus knew a great deal about the Essenes, claiming to have spent time with them. He said of the community: "The Essenes reject pleasures as an evil, but esteem continence, and the conquest over our passions, to be virtue. These men are despisers of riches, and so very communicative as raises our admiration. It is a law among them, that those who come to them must let what they have be common to the whole order, insomuch that among them all there is no appearance of poverty, or excess of riches, but every one's possessions are intermingled with every other's possessions; and so there is, as it were, one patrimony among all the brethren."

and stucco, several small inkwells were found, has led researchers to believe that the compound was, in fact, a kind of *scriptorium* where Essene scribes made copies of the sacred writings and of the rules and laws that governed the community. Many of its members may have lived close to Qumran for some time. At Qumran, they hosted community celebrations and events attended by up to several thousand people, who settled on the outskirts in tents, huts, and caves. It was in the latter, carved out of the marl cliffs close to Qumran, that the sacred scrolls and manuscripts were hidden shortly before the site was occupied by the Romans in 68 CE, whilst they were suppressing the Great Revolt. The site was permanently abandoned around 73–74 CE, when the Romans definitively deserted the Qumran garrison. The region's extremely dry climate preserved the texts, most of which were written on parchment, until they were discovered almost two thousand years afterwards.

Conspiracy to Hide the Scrolls?

Between the 1950s and the 1990s, a cloud of confusion hung over the slow publication of the scrolls. There was a series of confrontations between those in possession of the Qumran manuscripts, and those who were unable to gain access to them.

From the time that Roland de Vaux, a Dominican priest, assumed responsibility for managing the team of scholars examining the Dead Sea Scrolls for the first time, from the late 1940s through the late 1980s, it appeared as though there was intent to cover up one of the most important archeological finds in the history of the world. The lack of information regarding the translation of the scrolls' contents, the secrecy surrounding the number and location of fragments found, and the confrontations between Jordanian, Israeli, and US institutions and individuals concerning possession of the scrolls, all generated suspicion in international scientific and academic circles of an attempt to conceal the manuscripts. What did they contain that could not be made public?

What was preventing them from being dated? Why did some of the initial researchers believe the manuscripts were of ancient origin, whereas others took the opposite position? Did they challenge the accepted origins of Christianity? If they had been written or watched over during the lifetime of Jesus of Nazareth, did they perhaps speak of the protagonists of the New Testament in coded language?

A SILENT CHURCH

The Vatican, ultimately responsible for the international commission of researchers led by the Dominican priest de Vaux (the commission was initially made up of seven experts, and later expanded to fifteen), was silent. The Vatican emphasized the considerable difficulty the specialists faced in precisely translating and interpreting the thousands of tiny fragments found at Qumran, some of which contained just a few letters or words. Furthermore, between 1950 and 1960, new sections of parchment, many of them not identifiable, were found by archeologists, Bedouins, and treasure hunters, and ended up in private hands, intensifying the level of speculation. As of 1990, the team of experts had published just seven volumes of the *editio princeps* (the complete series, Discoveries in the Judaean Desert, edited by Oxford Press, contains forty volumes). Only a small group of specialists had access to the scrolls, which led to a great deal of suspicion. It is also worth noting that the turbulent political climate in the region at the time did nothing to assist the progress of the research.

Consulting the scrolls

Full access to the Dead Sea Scrolls was finally made possible in 1991 thanks to two events. Firstly, the decision of the Huntington Library to allow unrestricted access to the microfilm records it held of the scrolls. Secondly, the publication of *A Facsimile Edition of the Dead Sea Scrolls* by the Biblical Archaeology Society, authored by Robert Eisenman and James Robinson and edited by Hershel Shanks. Shortly afterwards, the Israel Antiquities Authority permitted free access to the scrolls.

FIELD WORK
Gerald Lankester Harding (in the foreground) and Roland de Vaux examine the ruins of the Qumran caves in 1958.

What Is Hidden Within Papyrus 7Q5?

If it is true that manuscript 7Q5, dated between 50 BCE and 50 CE, contains a text from the Gospel of Mark, this small papyrus would show that the Gospel was closer to the historical Jesus than has been believed.

The attributes of Cave 7 at Qumran differentiate it from other Dead Sea Caves in which manuscripts were found. It is the only cave in which documents written exclusively in Greek were found (in Cave 4, four texts in Greek were found, in addition to texts in Hebrew and Aramaic). It is the only cave in which papyrus scrolls were found (in the others, parchments were found). And it contained a text from the Syriac Apocalypse of Baruch, which did not appear in the other caves. Furthermore, the 19 papyrus fragments here were found inside an amphora on which was an inscription in black ink with the word "Rumah" ("Rome" in Hebrew). Nevertheless, the first researchers at Qumran paid it no special attention; perhaps because the texts here were in worse condition

than many others, which made it difficult to identify them. Initially, researchers identified fragments 7Q1 (Exodus 28:4–7) and 7Q2 (verses from Baruch from the Letter of Jeremiah), with the remainder classified as being of "probable biblical origin." That all changed in 1972 when Spanish papyrologist, José O'Callaghan (1922– 2001), professor at the Pontifical Biblical Institute of Rome and director of the Papyrological Seminar of Sant Cugat (Barcelona), published his own research

QUESTIONABLE IDENTIFICATION
O'Callaghan concluded that the four papyrus scrolls (7Q5, 7Q6, 7Q7 and 7Q15) contained text from the Gospel of Mark, which led to widespread controversy and, ultimately, cost him his authority in the field. However, some years later, German theologian and papyrologist Carsten Peter Thiede (1952–2004) endorsed the validity of O'Callaghan's

work. Professor O'Callaghan started by studying fragment 7Q5 (written in "Zierstil," a writing style used by the scribes at the time of Herod), which contained five lines with no spacing between words and phrases, and 20 letters. He scanned the texts of the Old Testament, but all his attempts to identify the text were futile, u[ ] tried with the New Testament. It was only then that he found the logical connection to Chapter 6, verses 52-53 of the Gospel of Mark, which states: (52) "for they did not understand concerning the loaves, but their heart was hardened. (53) And crossing over to the land they came unto Gennesaret and drew to the shore." The text in Greek contains 122 letters; the papyrus just 20. Of them, eight appeared to be in the correct position. However, in recent years, experts such as Dan[ ] Wallace have stated that the identification of the letters was not entirely correct.

What is the scientific consensus on the matter?

The oldest text found belonging to a Gospel is named P52, a small fragment (approximately 9 x 6 cm, or 3.5 x 2.4 inches) of a codex of the Gospel According to John. Using paleography, the fragment has been dated to the mid-second century CE, placing it one hundred years after the time when fragment 7Q5 from Qumran was written, identified by some as the Gospel According to Mark (seen below, in a Medieval setting). The scientific consensus, however, denies that there is any evidence of text from the New Testament in Qumran or at any nearby archeological site. As regards the texts in Greek found in Caves 4 and 7, experts like Emanuel Tov are only willing to confirm that the fragments contain passages from the Septuagint and the Book of Enoch, in addition to other biblical (canonical or apocryphal) writings, many of which are yet to be identified.

CONTROVERSY
The source of controversy, fragment 7Q5 (right) is a small, misshapen piece measuring just 1.5 x 1.1 inches (3.9 x 2.7 centimeters). It contains parts of words, spread across four lines. Some believe it is the oldest Christian text known to man.

Opposing theories

Despite the allure of the O'Callaghan-Thiede hypothesis, most biblical experts reject its credibility. Scholars like Professor Robert H. Gundry (an expert on the New Testament) and Daniel B. Wallace (Executive Director at the The Center for the Study of New Testament Manuscripts) published articles on the subject around a decade ago, in which they point out that identifying fragment 7Q5 as part of the Gospel According to Mark would call for several amendments in order for there to be consistency between the texts. Furthermore, in Wallace's opinion, the identification of the letters is incorrect in any case. An alternative approach suggests that 7Q5 may represent a tradition followed by Mark, but not necessarily the Gospel According to Mark itself. The fact that Cave 7 contained exclusively texts in Greek could give rise to the possibility that after Qumran was abandoned, it was used as a hiding place to store texts.

The Qumran *Scriptorium*

An elongated room stands out amongst the ruins of Qumran. It is known as the scriptorium ("reading room"), and it is assumed that copies were made here of some of the texts found in the nearby caves. If this were true, it would serve as proof of a link between the citadel and the caves.

SCRIBES
The scribes copied texts onto parchment under the watchful eye of a supervisor, who can be seen here cleaning an inkwell.

THE BENCHES
The tables and benches in this room (the second floor of Locus 30, as it was named by archeologists) indicate its role as a scriptorium.

Piacobino

The Origins of the Writings

The benches and tables (left photo) found by historian Roland de Vaux on the second floor of the scriptorium at Qumran are one of the archaeological finds that suggest texts were copied here. No scrolls were found, but inkwells and pots similar to those in the caves were discovered here. The ink inside the inkwells matched the ink on the scrolls.

DICTATION

One of the members of the community dictates a sacred text to a scribe. Members had to be in a ritual state of purity in order to carry out this task. The parchments themselves had to come from "clean" animals, and they were prepared adhering to strict rules of hygiene.

Infrared Imaging

Numerous scientific advances have facilitated a more in-depth understanding of the scrolls. In addition to conventional photography, which has allowed researchers to preserve the content of the scrolls before they deteriorate further, infrared imaging made it possible to see text that is otherwise invisible to the naked eye.

Thermal radiation

Visible light, just like X-rays and radio waves, is a form of electromagnetic radiation. Within the electromagnetic spectrum, which encompasses all such waves, the range visible to the human eye spans from red to violet or, technically speaking, wavelengths between 700 and 400 nanometers. Ultraviolet rays are a form of radiation that have a wavelength greater than violet. Infrareds, on the other hand, have a wavelength shorter than red. Infrared radiation, or thermal radiation, marks the heat emitted by a body. There are photographic filters that allow only infrared and ultraviolet light to pass through, facilitating the acquisition of images that cannot be seen by the naked eye.

ARCHIVING TASKS
Israel has launched a program to digitally photograph all the Dead Sea Scrolls, both in color and infrared formats.

CONSIDERABLE DIFFERENCE
When photographing a scroll using a camera with an infrared filter, the lens records the difference between the heat reflected by the ink and the parchment, offering a clear image with good contrast, whereas to the naked eye, the scroll's surface appears dark and illegible. This has resulted in a significant number of fragments being recovered.

WITHOUT INFRARED
The surface of the parchment that has darkened over time prevents a clear reading of the text.

Alternative Techniques

A wide range of tests have been performed on the Dead Sea Scrolls, not only to date them more precisely, but also using DNA techniques to establish where the parchments were sourced and produced. Developments in genetic engineering, particularly since 1985, has facilitated these studies.

PALEOGRAPHY
The study of ancient writing, which facilitates dating texts with varying levels of precision, analyzes the writing style and symbols used. This technique also considers the materials used in the texts.

Preventive methods

Today, researchers employ a series of techniques designed to minimize the gradual wearing down to which the scrolls are subjected. This includes working with sterilized gloves and special lighting. Furthermore, the scrolls are stored in temperature and humidity controlled environments, reducing the risk of deterioration.

yesterday: 1953

Gerald Lankester Harding examines a fragment whilst smoking a cigarette and without using sterilized gloves. Half a century ago, working conditions and techniques involved little care as regards preserving the texts.

today: 2006

The activities currently performed by scientists include removing cellulose adhesive tape (which deteriorates the parchment), with which the first researchers connected the fragments, from the scrolls.

WITH INFRARED
The text can be read with greater clarity. Infrared imaging was first used on the scrolls during the 1950s.

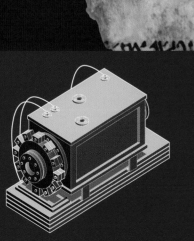

CARBON-14
Using Accelerator Mass Spectrometry, a more accurate and reliable frame is established for dating parchment and papyrus. This technique has served to support paleographic analysis.

DNA TESTING
Used to establish the origin and characteristics of animal skin (goat, sheep) from which the parchments were produced. This allows the different fragments of a single manuscript to be identified more accurately.

Where Is the Copper Scroll Treasure?

In 1952, in Cave 3 of Qumran, a very special scroll was found. It is not made from parchment or papyrus, but copper, and engraved on its two sheets are the locations of 64 places in Israel where great riches were hidden.

What is known as the Copper Scroll (3Q15) is one of the most disconcerting documents found in Qumran. It was found in Cave 3 in 1952 in poor condition. It was made up of two rolled-up sheets of copper, and the corroded state of the metal prevented the sheets being unrolled for analysis. In 1956 it was decided to cut the scroll into strips. The work, supervised by Briton John Allegro, fell to professor Henry Wright Baker of Manchester University, who cut it into 23 pieces with a circular saw designed especially for the purpose. Once it was opened, a surprise was revealed. The scroll contained a list in Hebrew of 64 places in Israel (in areas to the south of Hebron, in ancient Tamar; near Shechem; in Jerusalem; and near Jericho) where, according to the document, valuable gold and silver objects had been hidden. It was a map to an incredible treasure.

UNUSUAL WRITING

The scroll had been engraved, furthermore, in a totally unusual style of writing. Some paragraphs seem to be written in a Hebrew language 800 years older than the scroll, and others in contemporary Hebrew of the day, like the rest of the documents found at Qumran. It seems to have been made by someone who did not speak the language in which it was written (perhaps to preserve the secret of its contents), as it contains about thirty writing and spelling errors. Seven of the names of places that it describes are followed by capital letters in Greek (a total of 16 letters), the purpose of which are still a mystery

today. The scroll gives specific instructions, including names of places, cities, and streets, for finding a treasure that could amount to several tons of highly valuable gold and silver coins altogether (it has been valued at at least a billion dollars), and which holds immeasurable historical value. It specifies, for example, that "in the irrigation tank of Shaveh, at its mouth, there are 70 silver talents buried at a depth of eleven cubits," and that "in the cave that is near the fountain that looks like Hakkoz's house, dig 6 cubits. [There are] six bars of gold." The complete list of the treasure ends with the mention of a duplicate scroll which has been named the Silver Scroll, which supposedly contains additional details about the location of the sites. Archeologists and treasure hunters are still looking for it in the Israeli desert.

Where is the treasure?

None of the treasures named in the Copper Scroll have ever been found. This could be because the names of the places mentioned in the manuscript no longer exist. It may also be due to the deliberate obscurity of the text. Others think that the treasure was removed at some point within the two millenniums that have passed since it was written. Some have argued that the Copper Scroll may have only been a fraud of the era, a rumor created by the ancient Jewish people, that the scroll may have been engraved with the intention of confusing whoever might try to search for it.

HISTORIC MOMENT
Professor Wright Baker opening the Copper Scroll.

Was it the Jerusalem Temple Treasure?

The majority of studies agree that it is highly unlikely that the list of treasures on the Copper Scroll would be referring to the riches of a community such as that of the Essenes. Their code of conduct required them to relinquish ownership of property and live in extreme asceticism. However, it is possible that as a result of their forsaking of material goods, these same goods were hidden in different places, perhaps with the intent of them being donated to the temple or used for the community in times of need. It has also been hypothesized that it was the treasure of the Second Jerusalem Temple (a reconstruction shown below), although Jewish Historian Flavius Josephus, author of *The Jewish War*, claimed that the treasure was still in the temple when the Romans destroyed it. On the other hand, the Arch of Titus in Rome shows an image of the major objects and furniture from the Jerusalem Temple being taken through the gates of Rome to the Forum in a parade.

Findings in the Ruins

The excavations at Qumran have revealed an archeological treasure very valuable toward better understanding its inhabitants. But mysteries also arise: Why were vessels full of coins found in what was understood to be a monastic community isolated from the world?

Silver coins

The large amount of coins found in Qumran (along with glass objects and fine vessels) shows that the site had an active and flourishing commercial sector, which seems to contradict the austere image of the community there. Roland de Vaux found nearly 700 copper coins and in 1955 he found three vases completely full of silver coins. In total, there were 560 pieces. The mouths of the vases were covered with lids made of palm fiber. Most of these coins were minted in the city of Tyre (in modern-day Lebanon). One of the hypotheses to explain their presence is that they could have been donated by those who had recently joined the community. It is also believed that this could have been stored toward a Temple Tax which each Jew had to pay upon reaching adulthood. However, recent analysis of the coins introduced the theory that the set of silver coins could have been set aside toward payment to Roman troops stationed there or in nearby areas after they defeated Qumran.

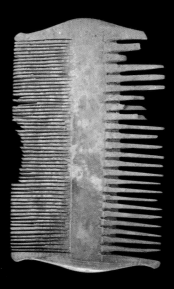

RITUAL VESSEL
The vessel is made of limestone (ritually pure) and measures 5.04 inches (12.8 centimeters) in diameter. It dates from the 1st century CE and is characteristic of those found in other sites from that era. Containers such as this one were used for ritual hand washings. The volume capacity of the vessel is that stipulated by Jewish law for liquids and solids.

DOUBLE-SIDED COMB
This object is made of boxwood and is two-sided: one for straightening hair and the other—with finer teeth— for removing lice.

SANDAL
Made of sheep hide. It is 8.66 inches (22 centimeters) long. The hide was usually dyed with vegetable derivatives such as nuts.

Manuscript vessel

A typical vessel from Qumran with the characteristic top, surrounded by other ceramic pieces. Vessels like this one were found in the caves at the site and had manuscripts inside them. At first, it was believed that this kind of container was unique to Qumran, but the same style of vessels have been found in nearby places, such as the Masada archeological site.

SUNDIAL
It is thought that this 7.5 inch (14.5 centimeter) diameter disc is a gnomon. It would have also been used to determine solstices and equinoxes.

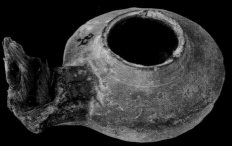

BEADED BRACELET
Small bracelet made of glass and stone beads with sizes ranging from 0.4 to 1.2 inches (1 to 3 centimeters). The bracelet is from the fourth or fifth century CE, so it corresponds to a period long after Qumran was inhabited.

OIL LAMP
This object was found with a coin inside and a palm fiber wick in the nozzle. The base was made with a potter's wheel while the nozzle was added afterwards.

BEFORE QUMRAN
One of the two silver scrolls (1.18 x 3.94 inches [3 x 10 centimeters]) found in 1979 near Jerusalem. Dating from the seventh century BCE, they contain the oldest known Hebrew biblical fragments.

Who Was the Teacher of Righteousness?

Several of the Dead Sea writings mention a "Teacher of Righteousness," a leader of the Qumran community who led his people into exile. Some hypotheses identify the teacher with individuals from early Christianity.

The Essenes established themselves as a community by the year 175 BCE, during the rule of Antiochus IV Epiphanes, king of the Seleucid Empire (successor of Alexander the Great). This Jewish group was opposed to the Hellenization being introduced in Judea, and so they went to the desert. The figure of the "Teacher of Righteousness" or "of Rectitude" would have emerged around 155 BCE with the purpose of leading the restoration of a theocratic order in Israel. In 152 BCE, Jonathan Maccabeus was appointed High Priest of Jerusalem, the head of the new independent Jewish kingdom that had conquered the Seleucids in 164 BCE. The "Teacher of Righteousness" refused to recognize this appointment, since Maccabeus was not a descendant of Aaron and was not from the House of Zadok. He therefore went into exile, taking a group of followers. It is very possible that Qumran was his chosen place of residence (he is often considered to be the founder of the local community), and he may have died there at the hands of an individual known as the "Wicked Priest" that some identify as Maccabeus himself. Recent analyses of the text show that there may have been several "Teachers of Righteousness" in addition to the founder, as a result of the title being passed down over generations

ORIGIN OF CHRISTIANITY

Some scholars have tried to link early Christianity with this leader that was venerated by the community of Qumran. Contradictory hypotheses have been proposed on the matter without much consensus in the scientific community: it has been said that Jesus was the Teacher of Righteousness and also that He was the Wicked Priest. With the finding of the Qumran documents and insight into their code of conduct, some researchers drew a series of interesting parallels between certain rites, institutions, and liturgy of the inhabitants of Qumran and Christianity. It is believed that the settlers of Qumran had a twelve member council forming a priesthood, and it is known that they ate together and gave the act a ritual significance since they considered the dining room to be a sanctuary; they prayed as a community; they practiced ritual and purification baths, as well as charity. The similarities, however, seem to be less significant than one may think: leading Biblical scholars assert that the differences between the Essenes and early Christianity are much more significant than the coincidental or vague similarities, caused by a common environment of this turbulent period.

HIGH PRIEST
The era of Qumran saw large clashes between Jewish groups.

HIGH PRIEST
The era of Qumran saw large clashes between Jewish groups.

Was John the Baptist a member of the Essenes?

From a historical perspective, it seems that the Essenes would have had more influence on the second generation of Christians than on Jesus or John the Baptist. They may have come into contact with the Essenism that spread through Palestine and in Jerusalem itself, rather than that of the community of Qumran. Some authors put forth that the similarities are not so much due to an entirely possible contact between Christians and Essenes, as much as to the fact that both sects come from a common tradition of Messianic Jewish resistance. It is also this similarity that gives rise to the hypothesis that John the Baptist was an Essene. His ascetic life leads one to consider him as such, although his call to civil powers and his message of conversion move him away from asceticism. John the Baptist could have been an Essene separated from Qumran who took a proactive approach to addressing the corrupt monarchy. The reality is that this theory can neither be affirmed nor denied. It is also a reality that both the Essenes and John lived in an ascetic environment and shared a common ideology.

Alternative Hypotheses

Is there a secret code in the Copper Scroll?

Within the Hebrew text of the Copper Scroll, which describes the location of various treasures, there are 16 Greek letters. An independent researcher (engineer Robert Feather, author of *The Secret Initiation of Jesus at Qumran*), joined the first 10 letters and was surprised to observe that they had formed the word Akhenaten (or Ikhnaton), the name of the "heretic pharaoh" of Egypt, predecessor and father of Tutankhamen. According to this author, Akhenaten was the first monotheist and the precursor to the monotheistic religions (Judaism, Christianity, and Islam). His name in the Copper Scroll could be seen as Jewish testimony recognizing the pharaoh, who lived more than a thousand years before the scrolls were written. Feather thinks that the Copper Scroll could have been a copy of a much older document, closer to the era of Akhenaten. However, there are no other mentions of the controversial pharaoh in the body of traditional Jewish writings. In addition to this controversial hypothesis, Feather also thinks that Jesus spent His formative years (regarding which the Gospels make no comment) in Qumran, where He was initiated in the community of the Essenes, making this community the nucleus from which Christianity emerged.

JEWISH PHARAOH
It has been confirmed that the name Akhenaten appears in the Copper Scrolls. It could be an incorrect reading, a coincidence, or something else.

Did the Church cover up the content of the Scrolls?

In 1991, the work *The Dead Sea Scrolls Deception* was published, authored by journalists Michael Baigent and Richard Leigh (best known for his book *The Holy Blood and the Holy Grail*, which proposes that Jesus was married to Mary Magdalene). In *The Dead Sea Scrolls Deception*, drawing on many years of silence from researchers as well as Robert H. Eisenman's thesis, the authors put forward that a handful of religious specialists, under Vatican control, conspired to hide some of the contents of the scrolls which would appear to undermine the principles of Christianity. In this work, the first section of which describes how the relationship among members of the expert commission deteriorated, the authors describe the scrolls, the preparation for their publication, the supposed consensus about them, and the problems that consequently arose. They maintain that a cover-up of the writings which are "compromising" to Christianity was intentional and directed by high echelons of the Catholic Church.

Are the texts written in code?

There is a series of manuscripts called *pesher* ("interpretation" or "commentary"), which consist of explanations of the Scriptures and which interpret them on two distinct levels of comprehension: one literal, for readers with limited knowledge, and one hidden, for those with a deeper understanding. Australian writer Barbara Thiering (1930) believes that the same method would have been applied to the Gospels later. Based on this theory, the author denies that the miracles in the life of Jesus (the virgin birth, crucifixion, and resurrection, among others) are real events. Instead, these references are considered fictions, constructed deliberately by the authors of the Gospels, with the object of symbolically disguising events of esoteric significance. Thiering's exegesis names John the Baptist the Teacher of Righteousness, while Jesus would have been the Wicked Priest; Jesus would have been married to Mary Magdalene, with whom He had two sons, from whom He would then divorce, to marry another woman. The scientific community does not share any of her views.

Did the authors of the Scrolls eat mushrooms?

In 1970, British author John Marco Allegro (1923–1988) published *The Sacred Mushroom and the Cross*, a book which engendered controversy and ruined his reputation. Until this time, Allegro had been a world renowned specialist in Semitic studies, linguistics, and Hebrew and Greek. He started working as part of the official Dead Sea Scrolls research team in 1953. He was in charge of translating the writings in Cave 4 (where the greatest quantity of fragments were found) and supervised the opening of the Copper Scroll. In both cases he published findings before the official editions were released. These actions generated friction within the translation team, and finally he was asked to resign from his position. After that, Allegro devoted himself entirely to writing. In *The Sacred Mushroom and the Cross*, the author proposes that the Essenes were the seed from which Christianity

emerged. He also affirms that various groups of Jews, among which the Essenes are included, followed a fertility cult with sexual rites, which included consumption of hallucinogenic mushrooms (*Amanita muscaria*). Although this work completely discredited him in the scientific community, some alternative researchers— such as Judith Anne Brown and Jan Irvin— have recently reclaimed his hypothesis.

JOHN M. ALLEGRO
The controversial British author was part of the select group of experts on the Dead Sea Scrolls.

Is the Last Supper an Essene rite?

Another supposed connection between early Christianity and the Essenes is the Last Supper. The document called *The Community Rule* mentions a priest that blesses the food and wine at a community meal, and the Rule of the Congregation of the Essenes mentions a meal which is presided over by two Messiahs. The French researcher Annie Jaubert (1912–1980) proposed that the dinner Jesus had with His disciples would have taken place according to the Essenian solar calendar. However, as already noted by the German Josef Blinzler (1910– 1970), it is not even certain that the Last Supper took place on the Passover.

NON-CHRISTIAN ORIGIN The Eucharist, as established by Jesus and as described in the Gospels, has similarities to Essene rites.

Were the Sadducees the inhabitants of Qumran?

Going against the academic majority, which attributes authorship of the Dead Sea Scrolls to the Essenes (or an offshoot of the group), Lawrence H. Schiffman, professor of Hebrew and Jewish studies at New York University, suggests that the writers of these scrolls were Sadducees who had fled during Herod's reign. According to what Schiffman writes in his article, *The Sadducean Origins of the Dead Sea Scroll Sect* (1992), the text called the *Halakhic Letter* (or manuscript 4QMMT) proposes laws of conduct virtually identical to the ones followed by the Sadducees. Fragments were also found in Qumran of a text already known since the nineteenth century as the *Damascus Document*, which also is considered to be of Sadducee origin (in fact, previously this manuscript was known as the *Sadducaic Fragments*). Lastly, in manuscripts pertaining to the community of Qumran itself, the community defines itself as "the sons of Zadok" (who was the high priest in Solomon's time and the source of the term "Sadducee"), the same self-description used by the Sadducees. Nevertheless, other beliefs and rites followed by the Qumran community directly oppose those held by the Sadducees. For example, the Sadducees did not believe in the existence of angels, the immortality of the soul, and resurrection. A possible hypothesis is that this sect of Sadducees had different beliefs than the principal group of Sadducees regarding these topics. Also it is speculated that the reference "Sons of Zadok" is simply a way to give prestige and legitimacy to the community.

Are there horoscopes within the Scrolls?

Although the Bible prohibits the worship of celestial bodies, such as divination through study of stars (or any other kind), there were astrological practices in the Jewish world (where stars are interpreted as being angels, not gods). Within the documents of the caves of Qumran, particularly Cave 4 (4Q186, 4Q534, 4Q561), writings with astrological themes have been found. These combine astrological information with physiognomy (the study of the personality based on the face and physiology of a person) to determine events and features in the destiny of a person. The underlying idea of this thinking is that the body (micro cosmos) is nothing but a reflection of the Universe (macro cosmos). To keep the text from being easily understood, the author wrote from left to right (the opposite direction of Hebrew) using a combination of languages: Greek, Hebrew, and Aramaic. One passage, for example, says: "This is the sign in which he was born: at the foot of the Bull. He will be poor; his animal is the bull." Another text (4Q318) interprets thunder to predict the future.

Are the Essenes fictitious?

A religion and Jewish philosophy professor, the Israeli Rachel Elior (1949), also thinks that the authors of the scrolls were Sadducees, but goes even further. According to her, the Essenes were invented by the Roman-Jewish historian Flavius Josephus. She holds out that he was inspired by the disciplined lives of the inhabitants of the Greek city of Sparta, and that the first author that mentioned the Essenes, Philo of Alexandria, was referring to a Utopian society, not necessarily a historical community. Elior indicates that there is no other mention of the Essenes, either in the Old or New Testaments, or in the manuscripts. Also, the professor affirms that it is inexplicable that a Jewish community practicing chastity has never been mentioned in any Jewish text, as it is a noteworthy characteristic, and goes against the Biblical law which mandates: "Be fruitful and multiply." Nevertheless, the idea that Josephus invented the Essenes is considered problematic, since Philo of Alexandria (who had been to Jerusalem) and Pliny the Elder both mentioned them.

PHILO OF ALEXANDRIA
According to Israeli professor Rachel Elior, the old Jewish historian wrote about a community which never existed.

To See and Visit

▼ OTHER PLACES OF INTEREST

MASADA
ISRAEL
A plateau located to the southwest of the Dead Sea, and the last bastion of Jewish defense in the first Jewish-Roman war. It fell to a Roman siege in 74 CE It is now a national park and was designated as a UNESCO World Heritage Site in 2001. In the early 1960s, Biblical manuscripts were found in the synagogue at the site.

ROCKEFELLER MUSEUM
JERUSALEM, ISRAEL
The museum opened to the public in 1938 and contains most of the Dead Sea Scrolls. Its extensive collection includes objects from prehistory to the times of the Ottoman Empire. It is the headquarters of the Israel Antiquities Authority.

JORDAN ARCHEOLOGICAL MUSEUM
AMMAN, JORDAN
Built in 1951, it is noteworthy for being the home of the famous Copper Scroll. The museum contains archeological artifacts of the region from the Paleolithic period through to the fifteenth century. Other nearby attractions include the statues of Ain Ghazal, one of the oldest settlements of the region (circa 7000 BCE).

MOUNT ZION
JERUSALEM, ISRAEL
The discovery of the ruins of the Door of the Essenes in the old wall of Jerusalem indicates that there was a Essene community south of Mount Zion, a very important place to Judaism and Christianity. In ancient times, the name given to a door indicated where it led to.

The ruins of Qumran

NATIONAL PARK
Today the area surrounding the ruins of Qumran is a national park which includes the cemetery beside the settlement and the nearby caves (included in the tour) where the Dead Sea Scrolls were found. It is one of the principal tourist destinations of the West Bank and Israel in general. The visitor center is designed to be a replica of the ruins, and one can view a documentary on the history of the archeological site.

TOURS
Tours last one or two days and depart from Jerusalem. The outings usually begin with the Masada ruins, continuing on to Ein Gedi, Qumran, and ending at Jericho. The journey from Jerusalem takes about 40 minutes. The visit lasts one or two hours. There is wheelchair access. This site is in the Judaean Desert, so it is important to wear light clothes, sunglasses, sunblock, and a hat, and to bring plenty of water.

OTHER LOCATIONS
Other interesting nearby sites are the Jordan River (where Jesus was baptized by John the Baptist) and the Dead Sea, valued for its curative properties and famous for being the lowest point on the planet (1,368 feet or 417 meters below sea level). It is also one of the bodies of water with the highest concentration of salt. The Dead Sea region has ancient Christian monasteries (such as Saint George's) carved out of the sheer rock cliffs.

The Temple of the Book

This is a wing of the Israel Museum in Jerusalem dedicated exclusively to the Dead Sea Scrolls. The exterior is made in the shape of the tops that were in the vases in which the scrolls were found. It houses the most complete and well-preserved parchments, among them the Book of Isaiah.

HUNTINGTON LIBRARY
SAN MARINO, CALIFORNIA, US
Has an original copy of the negatives of the Dead Sea Scrolls in microfilm, taken in 1980. Currently there is no public access to the negatives. There is also a large collection of manuscripts, a significant art gallery, and an impressive series of thematic botanical gardens.

AZUSA PACIFIC UNIVERSITY
LOS ANGELES, US
This Evangelical university acquired five of the scrolls in 2009 (in the US, the Oriental Institute of the University of Chicago has one and Southwestern Baptist Theological Seminary has three). In May of 2010, they were put on public display for the first time.

ORION CENTER
JERUSALEM , ISRAEL
Its complete name is the Orion Center for the Study of the Dead Sea Scrolls and Associated Literature. It is a part of the Hebrew University of Jerusalem. Established in 1995, it is devoted to promoting Dead Sea Scrolls research. There is a resource room to facilitate the work of specialists.

ANCIENT BIBLICAL MANUSCRIPT CENTER
CLAREMONT , CALIFORNIA, US
This center houses the negatives of the first photographs of the Dead Sea Scrolls taken by John Trever, similar to the microfilm copies from 1980 given to the Huntington Library. It has a complete catalog of the images, which is available to academics.

A Mystery for the 21st Century

Turín, 1898. The photographer Secondo Pia could hardly believe what he was seeing. Overcome by emotion, he states that he is the first person in 1,900 years to see the face of Jesus of Nazareth. What should be a photographic negative appears to be a positive, one that shows not only the face of Jesus, but also both sides of His body, with all the wounds of the crucifixion, and with a degree of detail that isn't found even in the evangelical accounts. With the photographs of Secondo Pia, the scientific study of the Shroud of Turin, or sindo-nology, was born. This still-unconcluded adventure continues to defy twenty-first century science, which has not been able to explain how the faint image of a man was transferred to the topmost fibers of a funeral shroud.

The Shroud of Turin is the most-studied object in history, and, despite this, we are still unable to decipher the mystery of the image of a crucified man appearing on its surface. We have witnessed multiple attempts to reproduce the image of the body, but in the end it has been impossible to produce an accurate copy with all the properties of the original image. The means by which the Shroud image was formed continues to be a mystery, and perhaps therein lies the great attraction of the shroud: we are capable of connecting with other people on the opposite side of the planet in a matter of seconds, but we still cannot explain the origin of the face whose gaze from the fabric defies us.

Sindonology, a term which has origins in the Greek word for shroud (*sindon*), and is preserved in the Italian *sindone*, includes numerous fields, from history and palynology to physics and photography. The history of the fabric alone carries us from Medieval Europe to the Templars, Constantinople, and the Byzantine Empire.

 The apparently infinite field of study means that it is very difficult to include all the various topics in a single work. It is also very difficult to write about the Shroud of Turin without falling into the trap of partisanship: usually either the author firmly believes in the authenticity of the Shroud and accepts everything supporting this theory without question, or they are convinced in advance that the Shroud, along with any relic, is a forgery, a product of Medieval superstition. Books that present both points of view, scientifically and accessibly, can be counted on one hand, and the reader has in their hands one of these works. There is nothing missing; everything is here, from the controversial carbon-14 dating and the heavily discussed and sometimes little understood work of Mechthild Flury-Lemberg in 2002 to recent attempts to reproduce the image on the Shroud by the Italian Luigi Garlaschelli.

Interpreting the various studies performed on the Shroud and the research into its history requires looking through a wide lens. Again, this book exceeds expectations: high-quality color images help explain to the reader the ins and outs of the Shroud, including a particularly good blueprint of how carbon-14 dating works, which honors the popular saying and is more understandable than a thousand words. There is also a detailed guide of all the distinct stains visible on the Shroud. While the Shroud is the most-studied relic from a scientific point of view, it is part of a network of other objects that are less well-known and, in many cases, have fewer claims to authenticity. The Ark of the Covenant (the item preserved in Axum, Ethiopia), the Holy Grail (with special reference to the Holy Chalice of Valencia), and the obsession of the Nazis with all of these objects complete this work, which hopes to impart to the reader in-depth research and knowledge regarding these enigmas.

Mark Guscin

Linguist, novelist, translator, and graduate in Classical Philology, University of Manchester. He has written books on the Sudarium of Oviedo and the Shroud of Turin and heads the specialized publication *British Society for the Turin Shroud*.

LAST EXHIBITION
The Shroud of Turin was the center of attention at the opening of its last exhibition on April 10, 2010.

The Holy Shroud and Other Mysteries

The Shroud of Turin is considered one of the most important Christian relics. To believers, this relic is the linen that was wrapped around Jesus' body after His crucifixion. To skeptics, it is only a forgery.

The Shroud of Turin, also called the Holy Shroud, the Turin Shroud, or the Sindone (from the Greek *sindon*, meaning a piece of fabric or sheet), is a rectangular piece of linen cloth that currently measures 174 x 44.5 inches (442 x 113 centimeters), although these measurements have been subject to slight variations throughout its colorful history. At first sight, the thing that grabs the observer's attention is the faint double figure of a human being, the face and front of the body on one side and the back on the other, that has faintly tinged the surface. There are also various triangular holes and stains denoting the passage of time and events such as the fires that occurred in 1532 and 1997. Nothing spectacular for a relic that presumably offers "scientific" proof of the foundational myth of Christianity: the resurrection of Jesus of Nazareth after being crucified by the Roman authorities in the first century. For centuries, the Shroud of Turin was a relic that concerned only believers. In 1898, on the occasion of the General Italian Exposition in Turin, a semi-professional photographer, Secondo Pia, was authorized to take the first photographs of the panel. During the film development process, Pia discovered that the negative showed, with a surprising level of resolution, the image of a bearded man with signs of wounds due to violence. Is this the authentic image of Jesus? Since the birth of Christianity as a religion separate from Judaism in the first century, relics and sacred objects became tools of great value for the hierarchy of the new belief system. In a violent and almost illiterate world, direct contact with anything related to Jesus and His Disciples (including dust from loculi, recesses where bodies were placed in catacombs) was useful to mobilize popular faith. The relics "guaranteed" protection against adversaries for those who possessed them and served to unite Christian communities, who were in competition with dioceses of Greco-Roman, Egyptian, and Mesopotamian origin. The first Eucharists were officiated on altars raised on or near the crypts and tombs of martyred saints. Later, these locations marked the places where the first churches were erected.

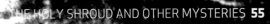

THE FACE OF THE MESSIAH?
This is the image that millions
of the faithful venerate as the
true face of Christ.

The Catholic Church considers veneration of the relics, together with visits to sanctuaries, pilgrimages, processions, the Stations of the Cross, religious dance, the rosary, medals, and so forth, part of "popular religion." Canonical relics are divided into three categories: bodies or body parts from sainted persons, including ashes and bones; objects that have been in physical contact with living saints or which have been sanctified by the same, from clothing to chains and other implements; pieces of cloth that have been in contact with relics in the first category, which are believed to have absorbed their virtues. Doubts have been raised about the authenticity of the Shroud of Turin since it "reappeared" in the fourteenth century. Those who identify it as the Mandylion (see page 63) track its journey from Jerusalem, passing through Edessa (now Urfa, in Turkey), to Constantinople, where it arrived in the year 944 and subsequently disappeared after the city was sacked by the Crusaders in 1204. The Shroud remained hidden for a century and a half. In 1349, the French knight Geoffrey de Charny requested permission to build a church in his duchy of Lirey where he could place the Shroud of Turin, which had fallen into his hands with no clear explanation as to how. He received this permission, and the Shroud was placed in this small village in Champagne in 1355. In 1389, Pierre d'Arcis, Bishop of the

nearby village of Troyes, wrote a letter to Pope Clement VII in which he asserted that "the Duke of Lirey, deceptively and fraudulently, motivated by greed, not out of devotion, but out of avarice, provided his church with a cloth painted through artifices (...), asserting that it was the same shroud in which our Savior Jesus Christ was wrapped in the tomb. And this was spread not only in the territories of France, but throughout the whole world, so that people from all over come to see it." Apparently, his predecessor in the office of Bishop had discovered the deception,

"the truth being attested to by the artist who had painted it." However, it is not certain that Pierre d'Arcis ever sent the letter, and he does not cite a specific name, and so the accusations of the Bishop seem to lose force.

The same Geoffrey de Charny was responsible for publicizing the return of the Shroud of Turin by organizing the first ostensions (public expositions of the relic), which attracted these "people from all over" who left their money in the inns and hostels of the towns lining the roads to Paris or other important capitals.

PRESERVATION OF THE SHROUD
Since its reappearance in the fourteenth century, the Holy Shroud has been stored folded (with the exception of public and private displays), in a silver reliquary, which was damaged in a fire in 1532 in Chambery. Since its arrival in Turin, it has been stored rolled around a wooden cylinder within a reliquary box, made of silver like the previous one. It was kept that way until 1997, when a powerful fire severely damaged the cathedral of Turin. It was decided then to take advantage of the situation to

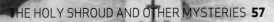

change the way it was stored. The accidental fire (the third recorded in the history of the Shroud of Turin), fed the faith of believers even more. The fire was noticed by the palace custodian, Giuseppe Ivano, close to midnight on Friday, April 11, 1997: "We began to smell smoke and then we saw the fire breaking through the dome," he later recounted. The rector of the cathedral, Francesco Barbero, was immediately notified, and issued the alarm to firefighters. The Shroud had been moved in early 1993 to a safer place within the cathedral.

PILGRIMAGE
The Turin Cathedral has been the Shroud's resting place since the end of the sixteenth century. Despite the controversy surrounding its authenticity, it remains the most important relic of Catholicism and attracts millions of pilgrims.

EXIBITION OF 1898
Promotional poster from the exhibition of 1898, during which the first photographs of the Shroud of Turin were taken, attracting the interest of the entire world.

It had previously rested on the altar, which would have destroyed the cloth, given the severity of the fire. In any case, while the fire remained out of control, the priority was to rescue the Shroud and put it in a safe place. A firefighter, Mario Trematore, grabbed a sledgehammer and began forcefully striking the 1.3 inches (39 millimeters) thick bulletproof glass. After a few minutes that seemed like an eternity, the Shroud was finally brought to safety, at 1:30 in the morning.

The Holy Shroud, which underwent a full restoration in 2002, is currently stored, stretched, in an urn made of light aircraft-grade aluminum alloy, with armored glass on the upper part, weighing almost a ton. Argon gas circulates through the interior with a minimum amount of oxygen, sufficient to guaranty the "breathability" of the cloth and that it does not suffer any type of biological or other contamination.

RELICS
The phenomenon of the relics spread widely as a result of the Crusades, an endeavor that had enormous religious,

Continued on page 60 ▶

Pilgrimage Destinations

Throughout the centuries, certain places have been the object of great displays of devotion by the Catholic Church and the Orthodox Church. Rome, Jerusalem, and Santiago de Compostela have been the most important as well as Istanbul, ancient capital of the Byzantine Empire and headquarters of the Orthodox Church.

Main Pilgrimage centers

Jerusalem, Holy Land
Vatican, Rome (Italy)
Santiago de Compostela (Spain)
Lourdes (France)
Lisieux (France)
Chartres (France)
Fatima (Portugal)
Istanbul (Turkey)
Mount Athos (Greece)
Assisi (Italy)

Santiago de Compostela
The cathedral is the burial site of the apostle James the Greater, according to Christian tradition. A pilgrimage center since the 9th century.

Vatican, Rome
Is the see of the Pope, the head of the Catholic Church.

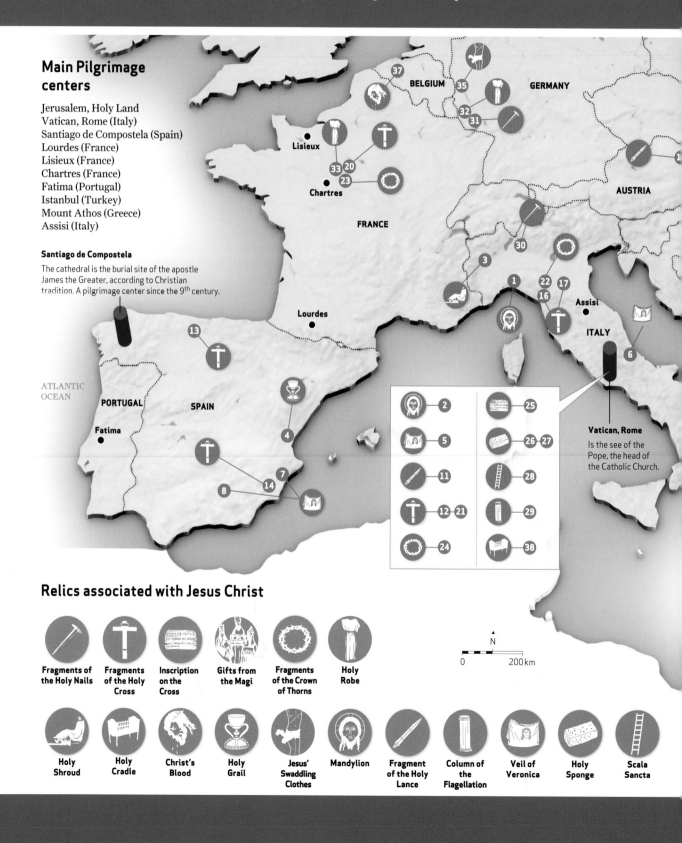

Relics associated with Jesus Christ

Fragments of the Holy Nails

Fragments of the Holy Cross

Inscription on the Cross

Gifts from the Magi

Fragments of the Crown of Thorns

Holy Robe

Holy Shroud

Holy Cradle

Christ's Blood

Holy Grail

Jesus' Swaddling Clothes

Mandylion

Fragment of the Holy Lance

Column of the Flagellation

Veil of Veronica

Holy Sponge

Scala Sancta

N

0   200 km

enigmas

Are there letters, in different ancient languages, hidden in the Holy Shroud?

When images of the Shroud were examined in 1979, the chemist Piero Ugolotti believed he saw a series of inscriptions around the face. It seemed there were Greek, Latin, and Hebrew characters. In 2009, French researcher Thierry Castex announced that there had been Aramaic letters among the Hebrew phonemes. Also, a group of scientists who examined the cloth with an image analyzer from NASA believed they saw signs of coins from the period of the Roman Empire on the images of the eyes.

References

1- Church of Saint Bartholomew of the Armenians, Genoa, Italy
2- Matilda Chapel, Vatican
3- Turin Cathedral, Italy
4- Valencia Cathedral, Spain
5- Saint Peter's Basilica, Vatican
6- Santo Rostro di Manoppello Church, Pescara, Italy
7- Santa Faz Monastery, Alicante, Spain
8- Asunción Cathedral, Jaén, Spain
9- Echmiadzin Cathedral, Armenia
10- Schatzkammer (Treasure Chamber), Vienna, Austria
11- Saint Peter's Basilica, Vatican
12- Saint Peter's Basilica, Vatican
13- Santo Toribio de Liébana Monastery, Cantabria, Spain
14- Vera Cruz Basilica, Murcia, Spain
15- Holy Sepulchre Church, Jerusalem, Israel
16- Pisa Cathedral, Italy
17- Florence Cathedral, Italy
18- Koutloumousiou Monastery, Mount Athos, Greece
19- Dečani Monastery, Kosovo

20- Notre Dame Cathedral, Paris, France
21- Holy Cross in Jerusalem Basilica, Rome
22- Santa Maria della Spina Church, Pisa, Italy
23- Notre Dame Cathedral, Paris, France
24- Holy Cross in Jerusalem Basilica, Rome
25- Holy Cross in Jerusalem Basilica, Rome
26- Holy Cross in Jerusalem Basilica, Rome
27- Saint John Lateran Archbasilica, Rome
28- Saint John Lateran Archbasilica, Rome
29- Saint Praxedes Basilica, Rome
30- Monza Cathedral, Italy
31- Trier Cathedral, Germany
32- Trier Cathedral, Germany
33- Argenteuil Basilica, France
34- Dubrovnik Cathedral, Croatia
35- Aquisgran Cathedral, Germany
36- Saint Paul's Monastery, Mount Athos, Greece
37- Basilica of the Holy Blood, Bruges, Belgium
38- Santa Maria Maggiore Basilica, Rome

KOSOVO
19

BLACK SEA

Istanbul

ARMENIA
9

18 36
Mount
Athos

GREECE

MEDITERRANEAN SEA

Jerusalem, Holy Land
Jerusalem is the Holy City par excellence for Christianity, where Jesus spent part of His life, and where the Last Supper and the Crucifixion took place. The Holy Land includes other important places such as Bethlehem and Nazareth.

15

In the Americas

-Nuestra Señora Aparecida Basilica, Brasil.

-Nuestra Señora de Guadalupe Basilica, México.

Mexico

Brazil

cultural, social, and economic repercussions. At the beginning of the twelfth century, hundreds of knights returned from the Holy Land to their homes in Europe with relics that were deposited in their parish churches, hermitages, and basilicas. These relics served to legitimize their authority and justify their military adventure. They also attracted pilgrims if the relic was considered very important. In Medieval Europe, there were virtually no churches without relics. It was not important that the fragments of the True Cross, the "holy nails," or the thorns from the crown multiplied, or that there were multiple examples of the Holy Lance used by the Roman Centurion Longinus to pierce Jesus in His side, or grails from the Last Supper. In Byzantium and the Near East, a rich artisanal industry had flourished, providing Europe with everything it needed. Monarchs such as Louis IX of France (Saint Louis) in the thirteenth century and Phillip II of Spain in the sixteenth century possessed extraordinary collections, which they enriched by paying vast fortunes for some relics. Authorized copies were also made, which were then lavished on illustrious guests by popes and monarchs and used to adorn newly-created Catholic temples. This practice is the reason that there are, for example, five replicas of the Shroud of Turin in the Americas: in the Dominican Monastery in Summit, New Jersey (United States), in the Monastery of the Ursulines in Quebec (Canada), two in Puebla (Mexico), and one in the Convent of Santo Domingo in Santiago del Estero (Argentina). And one cannot forget the other "Shrouds," entire or in parts, that are found throughout the entire European continent. Logically, if one believes in the Resurrection, it is impossible to find a corporal relic or bone fragment from Jesus. This has not impeded the multiplication of Holy Prepuces. In 1900, the Congregation for the Doctrine of the Faith, the Vatican institution tasked with maintaining the purity of the Catholic tenants, finally revoked the veneration of this object. Other objects have also proliferated, such as the Holy Tunic, in theory worn by Jesus during the Last Supper and torn off before He was hung on the cross. One such Tunic is venerated in Trier (Germany). Another, in Argenteuil (France). Controversy likewise surrounds Jesus' Swaddling Clothes, kept in Lerida (Spain), among other places, until being lost after the Spanish civil war.

HISTORICAL EVENT

When Secondo Pia obtained the negative image of the Shroud in 1898, he was accused of fraud. However, the Vatican received the news with satisfaction. In the June 14th edition of the official Vatican publication, *L'Osservatore Romano*, an article titled "A Miraculous Event" was published. The end of the nineteenth century was an especially difficult time for the Catholic Church. The bourgeois rebellions and the Industrial Revolution had limited its influence in European society, and the advance of agnosticism had brought into question, if not directly ridiculed, any tenet of faith. With the Shroud of Turin (property of the House of Savoy from 1453 to 1983), the Vatican believed they had a means to respond to their enemies. The Shroud of Turin paradoxically placed Ulysse Chevalier (considered one of the most learned men in France) in opposition to the canon, and Yves Delage, a professor of zoology, anatomy, and physiology at the Sorbonne, a recognized atheist, in favor of the same. The controversy intensified when, in 1931, Guiseppe Enrie took the second series of official photographs of the Shroud, which confirmed the existence of a negative image, undetectable to the naked eye. In 1988, the Holy See authorized an analysis of the Shroud using carbon-14, or radiocarbon, dating. Three independent laboratories (the University of Arizona, Oxford University, and the Polytechnic Institute of Zurich) performed the analysis, supervised by the British Museum. The result: the fabric had been woven between 1260 and

Ian Wilson
1941

Born in Great Britain, Wilson is one of the best-known writers and researchers of the Shroud of Turin. He achieved international fame in 1978 with his book *The Turin Shroud: The Burial Cloth of Jesus Christ?* In 1998, he published *The Blood and the Shroud*, and two years later *The Turin Shroud: Unshrouding the Mystery*, sharing authorship with STURP founder Barrie Schwortz. In 2008, he returned to the theme with *The Shroud: The 2,000 Year Old Mystery Solved.*

CONTROVERSIAL The first to raise the controversial hypothesis that the Image of Edessa (*Mandylion*) is the Shroud of Turin.

◄ *From page 57*

Continued on page 64 ►

The STURP Project

Concurrently with the 1978 exhibition (held to celebrate the 400-year anniversary of the Shroud's arrival in Turin), a group of 33 scientists was formed to study the Shroud exhaustively. The project was called the Shroud of Turin Research Project (STURP). Among its founders were physicist John P. Jackson, thermodynamicist Eric Jumper, and photographer William Mottern.

Nuclear physicist Tom D'Muhala was elected president. Other notable members included biophysicist John Heller and photographer Barrie Schwortz. The team worked for five days on the Shroud in October of 1978. They took photographs and samples with adhesive tape, and performed examinations under a microscope. In 1981, STURP released their final report. In their conclusions, the team explained that

they had not found traces of paint or pigments, that the blood stains were real, that the Shroud was not the work of an artist, and chemical and physical processes, performed in a laboratory, could have been used, giving rise to the image. These findings notwithstanding, they affirmed that, "there are no known chemical or physical methods that could have produced the entirety of the image."

UNKNOWN Despite the exhaustive studies performed by the STURP team, its members consider the creation of the image on the Shroud of Turin a mystery still to be solved.

Leen Ritmeyer
1945

An architect specializing in Biblical architecture, he has studied the sacred sites in Jerusalem and the surrounding areas for more than 30 years. He researched the location of the Temple of Solomon and its modifications and later renovations. He has also dedicated himself to the study of the Ark of the Covenant in Biblical times. His major work, *The Quest, Revealing the Temple Mount in Jerusalem*, appeared in 2006, and is the result of three decades of studies on the subject.

AUTHORITY Originally from the Netherlands, Ritmeyer is one of the utmost authorities on Biblical archeology.

Secondo Pia
1855–1941

Born in Asti, 34.18 miles (55 kilometers) from Turin (Italy), Pia was a lawyer who practiced photography, which was still in its infancy, as a hobby. He obtained permission to photograph the Shroud of Turin in 1898 and discovered, upon developing the large glass plates, that the negative revealed a much more detailed image than the positive. "I felt a strong emotion when I saw the Holy Face appear in the plate for the first time," he stated. With his casual discovery, he birthed the study of sindonology.

DISCOVERER Thanks to his interest in photography, Pia paved the way for the Shroud to generate controversy in the faithful and scientists alike.

Richard Cavendish
1930

British historian specializing in Medieval Studies. His primary research interests include magic and occultism, especially in the British Isles. Reclaiming the inheritance of classic authors such as Roger Sherman Loomis (who identified the Celtic origins of the Grail and its symbolic Christian roots), he analyzed the Grail in *King Arthur and the Grail* (1978). His major work is *Man, Myth & Magic: An Illustrated Encyclopedia of the Supernatural*, a work of 24 volumes.

MYTH RESEARCHER A distinguished researcher of the world of magic, he researched the symbolism of Arthurian and Grail legends.

Mark Guscin
1964

British philologist and translator, currently residing in Spain. He has studied and written books and articles about the *Mandylion*, or Image of Edessa, the Sudarium of Oviedo, and the Shroud of Turin. He translated to English a sermon given in the city of Constantinople in 944, in which a possible link between the Image of Edessa and the Shroud of Turin was established. He has criticized the theory that the Shroud contains writing in Greek and Hebrew.

SPECIALIST Guscin has written books and articles about the different pieces of cloth traditionally having a direct relation to Jesus.

The Route of the Relics

The Holy Shroud, the Holy Grail, and the Ark of the Covenant are the three relics that have generated the greatest fascination in the Christian faith. In each case, there are several objects believed to be the true relic of Jesus, and while there is no certainty, these are the possible paths they could have taken from Jerusalem to their current locations.

Extended area

Lirey

FRANCE

SWITZERLAND

Chambéry

Turin

ITALY

San Juan de la Peña
Monastery (8th century)

Zaragoza
(14th century)

Huesca
(3rd century)

Rome
(Saint Peter's)

SPAIN

Valencia
(15th century
to present day)

GREECE

ATLANTIC
OCEAN

The Way of the Holy Grail, a journey of more than 500 km between San Juan de la Peña and Valencia, was inaugurated in 2002 with the goal of promoting the Catholic faith and tourism.

MEDITERRANEAN
SEA

LIBYA

HOLY GRAIL

TECHNICAL DATA

- **Main Candidate:**
  Holy Chalice of Valencia.

- **Biblical reference:**
  Mentioned in the Gospels of Matthew (26:59), Mark (14:22-25), Luke (22:15-20), and 1 Corinthians (11:23-27).

- **Present location:** Valencia, Spain.

- **Description:** This is the name of a legendary holy receptacle, also identified as the Eucharist Chalice, used by Jesus Christ at the Last Supper.

- **Weight:** No data available.

- **Size:**

9.5 cm

7 cm

17 cm

14.5 cm

REFERENCES

- → Holy Shroud route
- → Holy Grail route
- ⤑ "Way of the Holy Grail"
- → Ark of the Covenant route
- ◉ Present location

N

0   500 km

What was the original form of the Holy Grail? Are we sure it was a cup?

In the classic tales of the knights, the Grail is described in vague and varying terms, possibly deliberately; it was only later that it was identified unequivocally as a single chalice, the one used at the Last Super and in which Joseph of Arimethea collected the blood of the crucified Christ. But in the tales, it is also described a plate or a tray (the word "grail" derived from the Latin *gradalis*, "wide and somewhat deep plate"), or as a rock fallen from the sky, generally an emerald.

enigmas

THE ARK OF THE COVENANT

TECHNICAL DATA

- **Main Candidate:** Ethiopian ark.
- **Biblical reference:** It is mentioned in the Old Testament in Exodus (25:10-21) and Samuel (6:1).
- **Present location:** Aksum, Ethiopia.
- **Description:** The ark was built at Moses' orders and its design was according to what Yahweh had ordered. It is believed that it holds the stone tablets on which Moses received the Ten Comandments.
- **Weight:** It seems it can weigh from 90 kg to 3.5 tons.

- **Size:**

0.78 m
0.78 m
1.31 m

A legend tells that king Abgar from Edessa (today Urfa, Turkey), received a fabric with the face of Jesus miraculously printed on it.
This image is known as the *Mandylion* or *Image of Edessa*. Some have identified it as the *Sindone*.

THE SHROUD OF TURIN

TECHNICAL DATA

- **Main Candidate:** The Shroud of Turin
- **Biblical reference:** The Shroud of Turin was first mentioned in the Gospels of Mathew (27:59), Mark (15:46) and Luke (23:53).
- **Present location:** Turin, Italy.
- **Description:** It is a linen fabric that shows an image in a photographic negative of a man with wounds and physical marks related to a crucifixion, as well as other unusual wounds that fit with the facts explained in the Passion.
- **Weight:** 1.42 kg.
- **Size:** surface 4.99 m².

4.42 m

1.13 m

Map labels

BLACK SEA

Istanbul

TURKEY

Edessa

CASPIAN SEA

ISRAEL
Jerusalem

IRAQ

IRAN

EGYPT

Elephantine Island

Mount Sinai (1500-1200 BC)

SAUDI ARABIA

PERSIAN GULF

RED SEA

SUDAN

Aksum (to present day)

Tana Kirkos Island (338 AD)

ETHIOPIA

Four miraculous images

Christian tradition includes a number of sacred images of Christ, but not all are the burial shroud that was wrapped around His body after the Crucifixion. It is important to differentiate the Holy Shroud from the Holy Sudarium (although in Spanish both names are used interchangeably to describe the Sindone). The sudarium was a towel used to wipe sweat from the face, and often covers the head of the deceased when the face was disfigured. The aforementioned relic is entitled the Sudarium of Oviedo (Spain), and does not have an image of Christ, but does have blood stains. Some researchers venture that these coincide exactly with the stains on the face on the Holy Shroud. Additionally, there is also the Veil—or Cloth—of Veronica. Veronica was a woman who, as Jesus carried the cross, dried His face with a cloth, on which His image miraculously appeared. This tradition, while recognized by the Church, is not found in the Gospel accounts, but rather originated during the Middle Ages. Churches in Rome, Spain, and France claim to possess the relic. There is also a legend that says that King Abgar of Edessa (today Urfa, Turkey), received a cloth with the face of Jesus miraculously imprinted on it. This image is known as the Mandylion (or the Image of Edessa) and is considered the first icon in history. Numerous churches assert that they possess the original relic. But that is not all: due to the lack of historical data and the confusing information provided by traditions and legends, the Mandylion has at times been identified both as the Holy Shroud and the Veil of Veronica.

CATHEDRAL OF OVIEDO
According to tradition, the sudarium that wrapped the face of Jesus when His body was placed in the sepulcher is found here.

The story of King Abgar

Abgar was a historical king of Edessa (today the Turkish city of Urfa), who lived during the time of Jesus. Armenian tradition considers him the first Christian king. The fourth century historian Eusebius wrote that this king exchanged letters with Jesus, asking Him to cure his illness. Jesus responded with a letter and sent one of His disciples to Edessa. In the fifth century, the idea arose that a painting was made of Jesus, commissioned by King Abgar.
Later, at the end of the sixth century, Evagrius Scholasticus stated that the image was miraculously printed on the cloth by Jesus to console the king. This is the Mandylion, which is often identified with the Holy Shroud.

TWIN COLUMNS
Corinthian ruins in the modern city of Urfa (Turkey), where Abgar reigned.

1390, which coincided with the first evidence of its appearance. Was this the end of the Shroud of Turin? Not at all. Reasonable doubts about the reliability of the test methods and the continuing appearance of scientific studies and articles leaning one way or the other (pollen analysis, photographic and physiological evidence, archeological research, radiographic projection) have kept the controversy alive.

◀ *From page 60*

This enduring reality is what differentiates the Shroud of Turin from other relics with a marked mythical or legendary tone, whose primary references are usually literary, or even cinematographic.

THE ARK AND THE GRAIL

That is the case with the Ark of the Covenant, in which the Jewish community preserved the Tablets containing the Ten Commandments that, according to tradition, Moses received directly from God. The Ark disappeared roughly 2,500 years ago, after the destruction of Jerusalem by the Babylonian king Nebuchadnezzar II. As for the Holy Grail, the cup used by Jesus to establish the sacrament of the Eucharist during the Last Supper, the most probable candidate is the chalice venerated in the Valencia Cathedral since 1437.

However, literary tradition has built, since the twelfth century, a truly pan-European cultural myth that has remained alive for centuries and far surpasses the sphere of the religious act. In contrast to these examples, the Shroud of Turin has the virtue of proximity. After ten years of silence, from April 10 to May 23, 2010, the Shroud was the subject of a public exhibition in the Cathedral of St. John.

GRAIL FOUND
Galahad, the perfect knight, is crowned king after ending the search for the Grail. Mural by the American artist Edwin Austin Abbey (1895), kept in the Boston Public Library.

The Shroud Markings

Whether a forgery or not, the Shroud contains a series of markings with distinct origins and from different time periods, which must be accurately identified for proper study. Some traces left on the fabric, however, continue to be controversial for researchers.

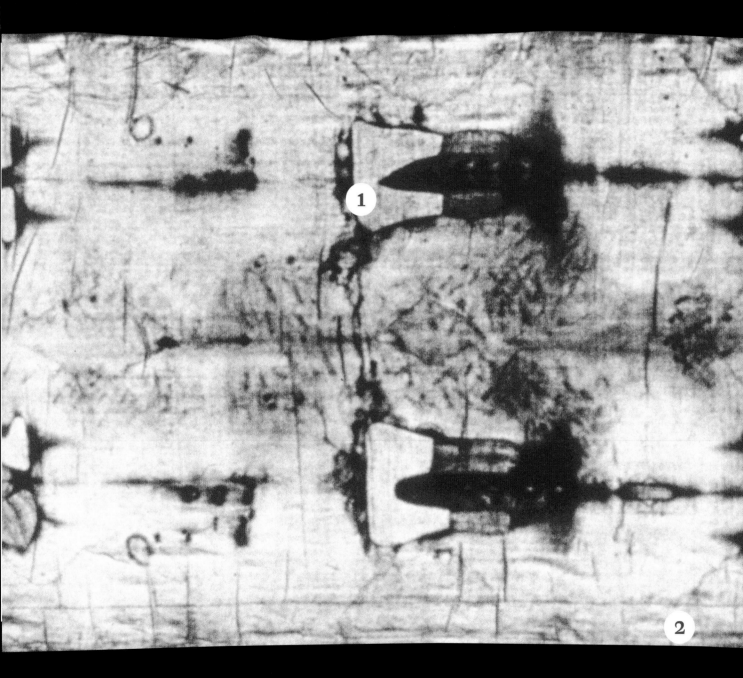

 FIRE
In the fire of 1532, a drop of melted silver burned one corner of the Shroud (which was folded), leaving a series of characteristic triangular holes. Two years later, patches were applied to the fabric. The L-shaped burns (on the left) occurred prior to this fire.

 THIN BORDER
According to some studies, a border along the length of the lower edge of the Shroud is a later addition. It still forms part of the Shroud of Turin, but during the 2002 restoration, directed by Professor Flury Lemberg, the 30 triangular patches sewn on by the Poor Clare Nuns in 1534 were removed.

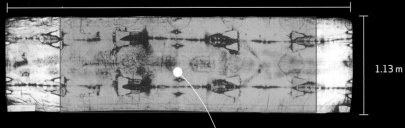

4.42 m

1.13 m

Preservation

A study carried out in June of 1998 suggested that the Shroud be preserved stretched out, rather than rolled or folded. It is found in a glass display cabinet (with laminated, bullet-proof glass) in a gaseous mixture of 99.5% argon and 0.5% oxygen, which maintains a steady temperature and humidity level.

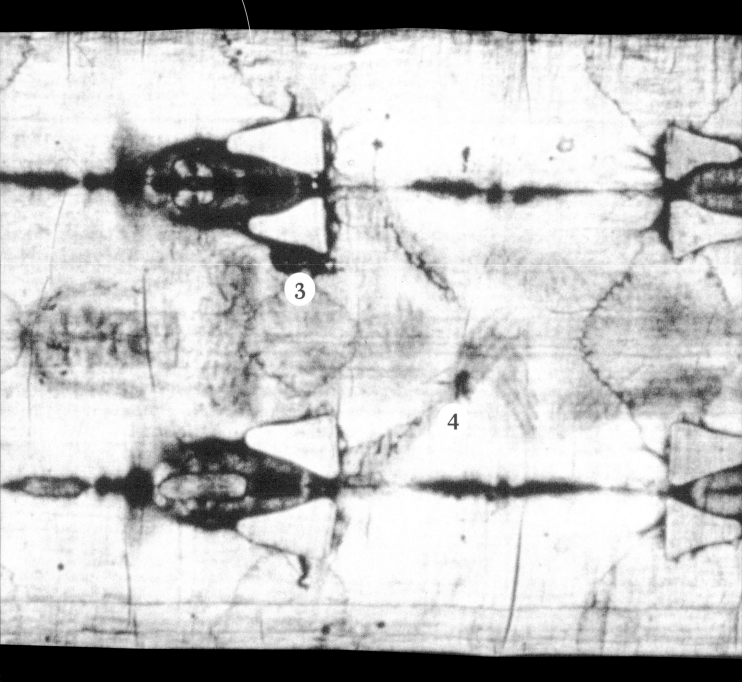

 BLOOD STAINS
There are indications of a large stream of blood on the front of the image, on the left side, where Christ traditionally was speared while on the cross. The stain spreads to the reverse of the fabric, onto the back of the figure. The face appears swollen, as if a consequence of blows suffered.

4 IRON NAILS
The arms are extended, with the hands crossed over the body. The right arm crosses over the left, and a blood stain is seen clearly on the wrist, caused by an iron nail. Blood stains also appear on the feet, caused by the penetration of another nail.

Relics of Christ

Throughout history, Christian devotion has motivated a number of relics associated with Christ, considered a support to the faith, to be preserved. Although science has revealed that many of them are not from the time when Jesus lived, symbolic value remains for believers.

The Iron Crown

Preserved in the Cathedral of Monza (Italy), this is one of the oldest royal jewels in existence (from the end of the sixth century), and was used by the Lombardian kings in their coronation. The Holy Roman Emperors, Charlemagne and Charles V, were crowned using this jewel, as was Napoleon, crowned King of Italy in Milan in 1805. Its name comes from the thin metal band circling its interior, made from a nail claimed to be one of those used in the Crucifixion. Traditionally, it is believed that Saint Helena, mother of the emperor Constantine, brought the nail to Rome from the Holy Land, along with a large number of other relics. The first historical references referring to a nail used in the Crucifixion being in this crown are from the sixteenth century. Based on tradition, the Church approved its veneration in 1717, regardless of the historical authenticity of the relic. Scientific examinations performed on the jewel in 1993 show that not only is the nail not made of iron (it is silver), it is from the mid-fourteenth century.

The Holy Nail

It is preserved in the Cathedral of Saint Peter in Trier, Germany, the oldest cathedral in the country. The Nail is protected by a richly ornamented reliquary from around the year 980. This relic was brought, like many others, by Saint Helena, the mother of Constantine. The Cathedral also possesses the Holy Tunic (worn by Jesus during His passage to Golgotha), the body of Saint Matthew, the sandal of Saint Andrew, and one of Saint Peter's teeth.

BLOOD OF JESUS
Preserved in the Basilica of the Holy Blood in Bruges, Belgium. According to tradition, it was collected by Joseph of Arimathea.

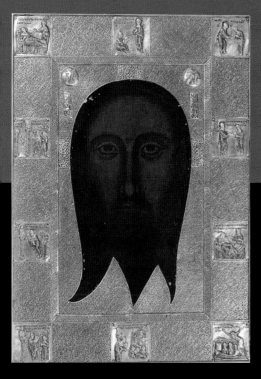

The Holy Face of Genoa

It is preserved in the Church of Saint Bartholomew of the Armenians in Genoa, and identified as the *Image of Edessa*, or *Mandylion*. The image arrived in Genoa in the mid-fourteenth century, and the frame surrounding it is from this time, though there have been no studies dating the image precisely. A similar relic also claims to be the historic *Mandylion*: the Holy Face of San Silvestro, today found in the Matilda Chapel in the Vatican Palace.

TITULUS CRUCIS
Part of the plaque on the Cross inscribed with Jesus' sentence. It is written in three languages, and the text (usually abbreviated as "INRI") reads from right to left. It is preserved in the Basilica of the Holy Cross in Jerusalem, in Rome.

LANCE OF LONGINUS
Also known as the "Holy Lance." Found in the treasury of the Hofburg Palace in Vienna. In 2003, it was dated to the seventh century.

FRAGMENT OF THE TRUE CROSS
Reliquary with one of the many fragments of the Cross dispersed throughout the world. This fragment is in the Basilica of the Holy Cross in Jerusalem (Rome). The Basilica has numerous other relics supposedly belonging to Christ.

How Did the Shroud Get to Turin?

The Shroud of Turin "reappeared" around 1355 in Lirey, a small village in France. Before this date, historical records have not been able to clear up doubts concerning its path. Since 1578, it has been found in the Turin Cathedral.

I n 1453, Margaret de Charny, widowed with no heirs, met with Louis I, Duke of Savoy. Her grandfather, Geoffrey de Charny, was responsible for the "resurrection" of the Shroud of Turin when, in 1355, he began to display the Shroud to the public in a small church in Lirey. In exchange for the Shroud of Turin, Louis I, Duke of Savoy, granted her a castle and its grounds and a pension. Years later, he also agreed to make restitution to the clerics of Lirey who had cared for the Shroud and demanded its return. The Shroud of Turin was linked to the House of Savoy for 530 years. In 1506, the Savoys moved the relic to the Sacred Chapel they had built for that purpose in Chambery (southeastern France). In December 1532, the Sacred Chapel was damaged by a fire.

The fire harmed the silver reliquary in which the Shroud was folded. A melted drop of silver fell onto the Shroud. Two years later, the Poor Clare Nuns repaired the Shroud. After various movements due to political instability, Emmanuel Philibert, Duke of Savoy, decided to move the Shroud permanently to Turin (Italy) in 1578, to the Cathedral of Saint John the Baptist, where it has remained, with the exception of sporadic absences for reasons of security. During the Second World War, it was hidden in the Abbey of Montevergine in Italy. In 1997, a fire destroyed the chapel at the Turin cathedral that had been the home of the Shroud of Turin since 1694. Luckily, the Shroud had been relocated in a display case behind the high altar three years earlier due to work being done. Thus it was saved. In 1983, Umberto of Savoy, the last King of Italy, who reigned for 33 days in 1946, died. His will transferred ownership of the Shroud of Turin to the Holy See.

UNCERTAIN ROAD
But where was Shroud of Turin before 1355? One theory defended by some sindonologists (researchers dedicated to the study of the relic) identifies the Shroud, as we have heard, as the Mandylion, or Image of Edessa (today in Urfa, Turkey). From there, it was moved to Constantinople. It is more difficult to trace its path after the sacking of Constantinople by the knights of the Fourth Crusade in 1204. Years later, Louis IX of France turned up with a "face" of Christ that could have been the Mandylion of Edessa. The Shroud then appeared in dozens of churches the world over. All were conjectures, until the sudden reappearance of the true Shroud of Turin in Lirey in the midst of the fourteenth century.

MIRACULOUS IMAGE
Painting from the tenth century showing King Abgar recieving the Mandylion, which has been identified as the Shroud of Turin by some.

The cause of the transfer to Turin

In August 1576, an epidemic of plague was declared in Milan. The city's archbishop, Carlo Borromeo, headed the fight against the plague, organizing assistance and selling religious works from the diocese to collect funds. When the epidemic was declared eradicated in January 1578, Borromeo decided to fulfill his promise to make a pilgrimage to the Shroud in Chambery to give thanks for the city's salvation. The Duke of Savoy, Emmanuel Philibert, decided to save the archbishop the arduous journey through the Alps and ordered the transfer of the Shroud to Turin. The Duke used the occasion to officially move the capital of the Duchy of Savoy to Turin, occupied several years earlier by French troops. This allowed the House of Savoy to reinforce its political position in Northern Italy.

Is the Shroud of Turin a Forgery?

Since 1898, two irreconcilable groups have faced off: those who assert that the Shroud of Turin is the burial cloth of Jesus, and the skeptics, who date the Shroud to the Middle Ages. The carbon-14 dating was the most decisive moment in this battle.

The photographs taken by Secondo Pia in 1898, as well as those taken by Giuseppe Enrie in 1931, were, for years, the basis for the first studies on the Shroud of Turin. The majority of these analyses were performed by adherents of sindonology, a discipline whose sole object of study is the Shroud of Turin, or Sindone. Studious skeptics argue that the absence of trustworthy historical documents establishing the existence of the Shroud of Turin before its appearance in Lirey in the fourteenth century is in itself a proof that the Shroud is a forgery. In addition, in December 2009, a shroud dating to the first century was discovered in the outskirts of Jerusalem. This discovery was very important, as the Jews buried their dead in a tomb sealed with a rock, and then one year later removed the remains to deposit them in a sepulcher; thus, until this discovery, no other shrouds had been found that could be compared to the Shroud of Turin. The comparison was made: the Shroud of Turin is a single piece, and is of a finer fabric, unusual for that time and place; the shroud of Jerusalem consists of two pieces, and, given its use, is of a coarser fabric. Strong evidence against the authenticity of the relic.

UNANSWERED QUESTIONS

However, some elements perplex those studying the Shroud, believers or not. The image on the Shroud of Turin is that of a man who has suffered wounds similar to those produced by a crucifixion, including the abnormal elongating of the forearms, and the lack of a visible thumb, turned under and hidden after the rotating of the wrist ligaments during the driving of the nail. If the wounds are to the wrists, why is Jesus always represented with stigmata on His palms? The scientific answer is that the standard representation is a historical error: the palms could never have supported the weight of an adult body. The Shroud is in agreement with history in this instance. Another frequently posed question is why the bearded image coincides so well with the Pantocrator found at the Monastery of Saint Catherine, on Mount Sinai (Egypt), from the sixth century, which is considered the basis of future iconic representations of Jesus. Was this Christ the model for the Shroud of Turin, or was it the reverse? These questions present strenuous challenges to science. In October 1978, at

enigmas

Is the Shroud of Turin the model for the Icons?

Sindonologists have highlighted the similarity between Medieval icons of Christ Pantocrator ("All Powerful") and the face on the Shroud. Fifteen similarities have been detailed, including prominent cheekbones and eyes, hair over the forehead, and a bifurcated beard. Researcher Ian Wilson indicates that it is significant that the first icon of this type that has been preserved (below, compared to the face on the Shroud) is from the sixth century, approximately the same time at which the Shroud reappeared (identified here as the *Mandylion*) on the historical radar. Skeptics believe, in contrast, that the influence has been the reverse, from the icons to the Shroud.

Is there a second face?

During the restoration of the Shroud in 2002, the rear section of the Shroud was scanned for the first time. In 2004, Giulio Fanti (photo), professor of Mechanical Engineering at the University of Padua, confirmed that the image of a second face had been found. According to Fanti, this image, an 85% match with the front, could have been created by the "corolla effect," an electrical discharge that, according to believers, could have occurred as a side effect of the Resurrection phenomenon.

the end of a public exhibition in Turin, several STURP (Shroud of Turin Research Project) researchers were given five days to perform, for the first time, scientific studies directly on the fabric of the Shroud. One group of these scientists claimed to have verified the presence of blood remnants.

MICROSCOPIC RESEARCH

A discordant voice, Walter McCrone, in contrast, sustained that there were traces of ochre red and vermilion paint on some fibers, which supports the forgery theory. Both pigments were very common during the Middle Ages, and would have been used to paint the body (ochre red) and to represent blood (vermilion). McCrone also referred to the existence of a book from 1847 titled *General Painting Techniques During the Fourteenth Century*, which described methods used to create diffuse images, such as that on the Shroud. McCrone performed his studies using a method called polarized light microscopy, capable of analyzing minute particles of fabric. Other researchers, in turn, asserted that the paint remnants were so minimal that they could have been the result of exterior contamination. In 1988, The Archdiocese of Turin agreed to perform a carbon-14 dating procedure, or radiocarbon dating, which measures the loss of molecules of this element in animals and plants after their deaths. Theoretically, a sure scientific proof. In April of that year, several samples of the Shroud's fabric were taken and sent to three diffe-

Similarity to the Pray Codex

The Pray Codex is preserved in Budapest, at the National Hungarian Library. It contains the first known text in Hungarian. It is estimated that the documents making up the Pray Codex were written between 1192 and 1195. It includes two illustrations that reflect both episodes after the crucifixion of Jesus. The first shows the anointing of the body, with strong parallels to the image on the Shroud of Turin: longer forearms than normal, thumbs that are not visible, and three marks on the forehead. The second shows an angel announcing the resurrection to the women who had gone to collect the body of Jesus in the tomb. At their feet is an empty Shroud, on which fabric threads and four small circles forming an "L" can be distinguished, which correspond to those found on the Shroud of Turin, and which were there prior to the fire of 1532. For defenders of the Shroud of Turin, this proves that, at the end of the twelfth century, the Shroud was already known.

HOLES
The Shroud has holes made by burns. How these came to be is unknown. There are four L-shaped holes, which indicates that the Shroud was folded in four sections.

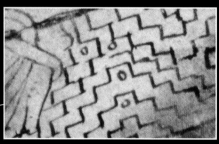

DETAIL
The Medieval illustration reveals a surprising similarity to the Shroud of Turin.

rent laboratories: the University of Arizona, Oxford University, and the Federal Polytechnic School of Zurich. Various leaks to the press (used to discredit the analysis) resulted in a large press conference at which the results were announced: the original date of the fabric from the Shroud of Turin "with a confidence level of 95 percent, is between the years 1260 and 1390."

POSSIBLE CONTAMINATION

However, many sindonologists criticized the lack of discretion during the process and argued that the analyses performed were imprecise due to various defects, the primary defect being that the fabric samples did not come from the original Shroud, but from the bits of Medieval fabric added during some repair, which, in addition, had been "contaminated" throughout the centuries. In 2008, a group of researchers from the Los Alamos National Laboratory (United States) verified that they had found cotton fibers in other samples from the same area

The pollen wars

In 1973 and 1978, Swiss criminalist and forensic scientist Max Frei-Sulzer took samples of what seemed to be traces of plant matter on the Shroud. He came to the conclusion that the pollen found documented the Shroud's presence in Palestine in the first century. Frei's reputation was tarnished in 1983, the year he died: he had verified the authenticity of Hitler's secret diaries, which were in fact forgeries. In 1998, the Israeli Avinoam Danin vindicated Frei's theory in part, despite the fact that the majority of specialists continue to oppose these conclusions.

CONTROVERSIAL
Max Frei-Sulzer taking samples from the Shroud of Turin. His conclusions were ruled precipitous and lacking scientific rigor.

21st century Shroud

In October 2009, Luigi Garlaschelli, a professor of Organic Chemistry at the University of Pavia (Italy), made a replica of the Shroud of Turin using elements and technology from the fourteenth century. He used an open-weave linen fabric with a herringbone pattern to emulate the original fabric. Following the theory set forth by skeptic Joe Nickell in 1983, he unrolled the fabric over a volunteer, applying ochre paint with acid based pigments over him. The resulting image was touched up by hand using a chemical substance based on sulfuric acid. Before adding the blood stains, the fabric was aged in an oven at 419°F (215°C) for three hours. Finally, it was washed to accentuate the blurring. Among the critiques his experiment has received is the fact that the faint image lacks the tridimensionality of the original.

SKEPTIC
Garlaschelli considered his experiment recreating the Shroud of Turin a success.

the test samples were taken from in 1988, which, in their estimation, annulled the carbon-14 dating. The only replication possible would be a new analysis, but the Holy See has rejected this because of the destructive effect that it would have on the fibers. The Vatican's position is that the Shroud of Turin must remain just as it is. If the Shroud of Turin is Medieval, then the image it contains must also be. So, how was it made? Some researchers who believe in the Shroud's authenticity speak of spontaneous nuclear radiation and great force, which imprinted the image (which does not in reality have the properties of a photographic negative) on the topmost layers of the fabric. This is the theory of French biophysicist Jean-Baptiste Rinaudo. This fits with a hypothetical "resurrection." Some skeptics say the image is the result of the first photograph in history, taken with a rather large and obscure artisanal camera (thus explaining the slight physical deficiencies in the image). But why is there nothing similar until the nineteenth century? Others think it was made with a technique similar to a copy using bas-relief molds, in this case a human body, combined with the use of acidic pigments and the degrading effects of the passage of time and various contaminating agents.

Carbon-14 dating

Developed in 1949 by Willard Libby (1970 Nobel Prize Winner in Chemistry) and perfected in 1977 with the creation of accelerator mass spectrometry, radiocarbon or carbon-14 dating is a very reliable method to measure organic residue up to 60,000 years old, although it is not infallible.

Carbon Loss

All organisms absorb carbon during their lifetimes; after death, the organic remains lose carbon in a regular and constant way, so that we can date the time when they lived. Accelerator mass spectrometry (AMS) allows us to analyze very small samples.

WHAT IS AN ISOTOPE?

Isotopes are atoms that have the same number of protons, but different numbers of neutrons. Carbon has 3 isotopes: ^{12}C, ^{13}C and ^{14}C. Carbon-14 is radioactive, as it disintegrates over time. This molecule appears in the remains of organic beings, and permits the dating of material up to 60,000 years old.

ION SOURCE

Allows for the study of molecules that are present in the samples (fibers). To achieve this, the samples are vaporized to provoke the release of their ions and a spectrum is shown through the detector that indicates the ions that make up the molecule in relation to their charges.

1 IONIZATION OF THE SAMPLE

Achieved by bombardment with electrons. This is done with cesium, which confers its electrons to the sample, obtaining negative carbon iions. The result of this physical phenomenon is a plasma which is induced through the duct.

Ion preaccelerator:
Directs the carbon ions

Duct

Ion beam

$^{12}C^-$

$^{13}C^-$

2 MAGNETIC DEFLECTOR

When the first separation from the negative ions has taken place, alternating mass equivalents are injected. The carbon-14 ions and the hydrogen-carbon molecules (methine and methylene) are induced toward the accelerator. The remaining particles are diverted and blocked by the magnetic device.

Electric lenses:
Focus the ion beam

THE HOLY SHROUD

For the dating of the Holy Shroud of Turin, laboratories were selected from three universities: University of Arizona, Oxford University, and the Federal Polytechnic School of Zurich. The sample consisted of a 2.76-inch (7-centimeter) piece of cloth, divided into three parts, weighing 50 mg each. The entire process was supervised by experts from the British Museum. The image on the right shows the size of the samples, but does not indicate its extraction location.

Sample size

Other Methods

Elements can also be dated using other scientific techniques.

Dendrochronology

Dating based on tree rings. ach tree produces one ring per year, with different thicknesses based on climatic conditions. This method is very precise, but only works to calculate up to 10,000 years ago.

Rehydroxylation

Works for dating pieces of ceramic. The technique permits the measurement of the amount of water that the elements of the clay have reabsorbed since they were baked for the first time, thereby revealing precisely when they were made.

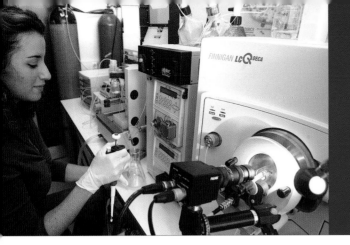

Dating problems

One inconvenience of the method is that it assumes the production of carbon-14 in the atmosphere has been constant for the last 60,000 years. However, there have been fluctuations in different eras and places that must be considered. In addition, samples may have been contaminated after the death of the living being, leading to the item being dated as younger than the real age.

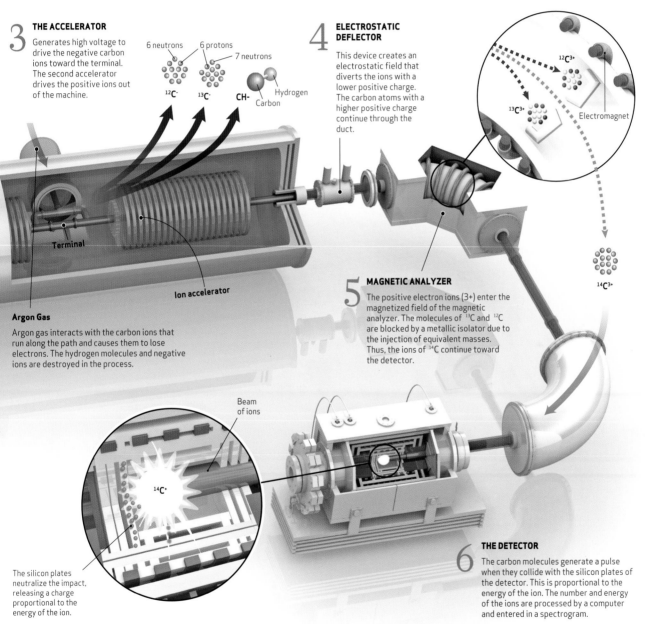

3 THE ACCELERATOR

Generates high voltage to drive the negative carbon ions toward the terminal. The second accelerator drives the positive ions out of the machine.

6 neutrons   6 protons   7 neutrons

$^{12}C^-$ $^{13}C^-$ CH^- Hydrogen   Carbon

Terminal

Ion accelerator

Argon Gas

Argon gas interacts with the carbon ions that run along the path and causes them to lose electrons. The hydrogen molecules and negative ions are destroyed in the process.

4 ELECTROSTATIC DEFLECTOR

This device creates an electrostatic field that diverts the ions with a lower positive charge. The carbon atoms with a higher positive charge continue through the duct.

$^{12}C^{3+}$ $^{13}C^{3+}$ Electromagnet

$^{14}C^{3+}$

5 MAGNETIC ANALYZER

The positive electron ions (3+) enter the magnetized field of the magnetic analyzer. The molecules of ^{13}C and ^{12}C are blocked by a metallic isolator due to the injection of equivalent masses. Thus, the ions of ^{14}C continue toward the detector.

Beam of ions

$^{14}C^+$

The silicon plates neutralize the impact, releasing a charge proportional to the energy of the ion.

6 THE DETECTOR

The carbon molecules generate a pulse when they collide with the silicon plates of the detector. This is proportional to the energy of the ion. The number and energy of the ions are processed by a computer and entered in a spectrogram.

Potassium-Argon

Similar to radiocarbon dating, this is based on the radioactive disintegration produced by the gradual change of the isotope potassium 40 in argon 40. It allows dating of rocks up to 5 million years old, but not less than 100,000 years old.

Uranium 238

adiometric system, also called fission track dating. This method allows for the dating of materials up to thousands of millions of years, which permits speculation about the origin of the arth and the solar system.

Thermoluminescence

Measures the radiation emitted by the crystal structure of inorganic material, such as ceramics, in a temporal range similar to carbon-14. One of its problems is that the margin of error is broad.

What Powers Are Attributed to the Holy Grail?

The Holy Grail is one of the most significant European myths of the Middle Ages, with Christian, Celtic, and Oriental roots. Was it really the chalice from the Last Supper? A relic, or a source of nearly divine power?

The myth begins when Joseph of Arimathea arrives on the English coast. In Glastonbury, he erected the first church in Great Britain, and decided to shelter inside it the chalice with which, according to tradition, he had collected the blood of Jesus on the cross, and which had previously been used to establish the sacrament of the Eucharist at the Last Supper: the Holy Grail. That is the story told in some medieval ballads from the late twelfth century and later decades. In another narrative, the Grail is found in a castle on Montsalvat mountain ("Mountain of Salvation"), whose king, the Fisher King, suffers an incurable wound waiting for the knight who asks the appropriate question: "Whom does the Grail serve?" That knight, Percival, asks the question and begins a new Golden Age in the region. The figure of Percival links the tradition of the Grail with the literary period dedicated to King Arthur. Lancelot, Gawain, Percival, and Galahad become mythical heroes throughout Europe.

MORE THAN A LEGEND?

In Arthurian legends, the Grail was seen as an allegory for spiritual illumination, based on a chivalrous code based on purity. In these narratives, the chalice had supernatural properties: it could cure the ill and rejuvenate people, as well as granting prosperity to those who possessed it and to their surrounding environment. To the contrary, those who were not worthy of approaching the Grail suffered a terrible fate, such as blindness, or even death, when they touched the relic. Despite the legendary origin, enriched by medieval literature, many believed there was a historical and literal background for these magical powers of the cup of Christ. The medieval ballads, which were explicitly Christian, incorporated elements of Celtic, German, and Scandinavian myths. They were enriched by Oriental mysticism, a fruit of the cultural exchange brought about by the Crusades as well as contact with the Jewish Kabbalah and Sufism, and possibly with other Oriental beliefs. Some identify the Grail with the magical Celtic cauldron. Others, with the relic-talisman of great powers that was in the possession of the Cathars. Or, with the true message of Christ, ethereal and symbolic, that had been entrusted to Joseph of Arimathea. Only fictional characters like Indiana Jones saw their efforts rewarded with finding the elusive chalice; in real life, however, searches have never yielded positive results.

LEGENDARY CHALICE
Percival with the Grail, late thirteenth century representation.

enigmas

Is the Grail in Valencia?

According to the Catholic Church, it is "completely plausible" that the Holy Chalice used by Jesus Christ at the Last Supper may be a small cup of polished agate found in the Cathedral of Santa Maria in Valencia (Spain). This cup, of Oriental origin, has been dated—so far, without challenge—to between 100 and 50 years before Christ, therefore it could have been in Jerusalem during the time of the Passion. Its modest dimensions 2.76 inches (7 centimeters) were enhanced with the addition of handles and a stem of engraved gold. Differing from the Arthurian legend of the Grail, it is believed that it arrived on the Iberian Peninsula in the third century in the hands of the deacon Saint Lorenzo. After a long journey, the King of Aragon, Alfonso V the Magnanimous, brought it to the cathedral in Valencia, where it was placed in the reliquary in 1437. Since 1916 it has been exhibited in the Chapel of the Holy Chalice.

Why Did the Nazis Covet the Grail?

Influenced by the neo-paganism that flourished during the first third of the Twentieth Century, the leaders of the Nazi party wanted to create their own mythology. The search for the Holy Grail attempted to legitimize the Aryan race as the true heirs of Christ.

After the German defeat in the First World War and the humiliation of the Treaty of Versailles (1919), there was a proliferation of pan-Germanic organizations, such as the Thule Society and the Vril Society, who wanted to build a mythology with one hundred percent national roots. They were also interested in integrating the Holy Grail into their doctrine, which established some of the basic theories of Naziism. Among the Nazi leaders interested in the Grail myth, Heinrich Himmler, head of the feared SS, stands out. Himmler thought that the Holy Grail was a physical object, a type of talisman with supernatural powers that would allow the Aryan people (the "pure" Germans) to take their place at the head of an old Europe decimated by two thousand years of Judeo-Christianity. Himmler entrusted the search for the Holy Grail to the Medieval scholar Otto Rahn, who was convinced that it had remained in France under the custody of the Cathars (a medieval heretic sect with its epicenter in the Languedoc region). To Rahn, the Montsegur castle, the last bastion of the Cathars which fell in 1244, was the Montsalvat that Wolfram von Eschenbach described in his *Parzival*.

SECOND ATTEMPT

After the mission's failure and the subsequent mysterious death of Rahn, Himmler entrusted the mission, still in secret, to colonel Otto Skorzeny, head of command, who in 1943 had rescued Mussolini from his Italian prison. According to the writer Howard Buechner, in 1944 Skorzeny ended up finding a treasure of thousands of coins and some mysterious tablets with indecipherable writing, and it was speculated that they could be the Tablets of the Ten Commandments. But Skorzeny died in Madrid in 1975 and never referred to this hypothetical mission while he was alive. Previously, on October 23, 1940, with the cover of a meeting that Adolf Hitler and the Spanish dictator Francisco Franco held in Hendaye, on the French-Spanish border, Himmler and some of his nearest aides moved to the Benedictine abbey of Montserrat, near Barcelona, another of the sacred mountains identified with Montsalvat. They found no sign of the precious relic in Montserrat. Before leaving, Himmler made clear the reason for his interest in the Grail: the Nazis, manipulating the Biblical legend of the twins Jacob and Esau, argued that the Aryan race was descended from the former, God's chosen, and the Jews from the latter. The Holy Grail, symbol of divine power, should be under the protection of the new Messiah, that is, Adolf Hitler.

Otto Rahn

Between 1929 and 1932, a young German who spoke the local dialect fluently was searching in Languedoc (France) for the whereabouts of the Holy Grail, which he thought had been in the possession of the heretic Cathars before they were annihilated at the beginning of the thirteenth century. This young man was Otto Rahn, who in 1933 authored the book *Crusade Against the Grail*. Its publication led to him being summoned by Heinrich Himmler, head of the SS. Rahn agreed to join the SS to, under their protection, continue with the mission to which he had dedicated his life. Having fallen into disgrace with the Nazi party (Rahn was openly homosexual), he died in 1939, at the age of 35. It appears he froze to death while performing the *endura*, a Cathar suicide rite that involved self-imposed starvation.

CATHAR REFUGE
Montsegur Castle, in the south of France. Rahn believed that he would find the Grail hidden there.

The crypt of the SS

Spurred on by his obsession, Himmler built a true temple devoted to the Aryan culture in the Wewelsburg Castle, located in central-west Germany. This Renaissance-style castle was built at the beginning of the seventeenth century. In 1934, Himmler took possession of the building, which he planned to convert into a study center for the SS. Although he never achieved this, he did make some renovations to convert it into the "new world center" the Nazi intelligentsia imagined. The numerous study rooms had epic names, such as "King Arthur Hall" or "Grail Hall." Various works of art that shared the Nazi aesthetic were incorporated, a task that fell to the Ahnenerbe ("Society for the Study and Teaching of German Ancestral Heritage"). The most spectacular changes in the castle, however, were made in the north tower. There, two new rooms were created: what was called the Hall of Generals, which had a mosaic of a "Black Sun" —mystic symbol of the SS, similar to a swastika, but with 12 arms—and the Crypt (image above). It is a circular enclosure with 12 niches, reminiscent of King Arthur's Round Table. There is a large swastika in the dome vault. In the center of the hall, a space was left empty, and prominent, for the Grail—a weapon that would be definitive in the great battle between Europe and the barbarians that, according to Himmler, was approaching.

MYSTICAL MANIA
A fervent follower of occult beliefs, Himmler (right) searched for—but did not find—the Grail.

Where Is the Ark of the Covenant Hidden?

According to the Bible, the Ark is a tangible and sacred object. Inside it were kept the Tablets of the Law received by Moses on Sinai. They are the symbol of the pact between Yahweh and the Jewish people. For 2,500 years the Ark's whereabouts have been unknown.

I n 586 BCE, Nebuchadnezzar II the Great, the Chaldean king of Babylon, conquered Jerusalem. The temple and all the sacred objects that were housed within it were sacked or destroyed. The most important item was the Ark of the Covenant, which, according to Exodus, had been commissioned by Moses according to the command of Yahweh (God) Himself on Mount Sinai. It was a box of acacia wood covered in gold, 4.2 feet (1.31 meters) wide and 2.5 feet (.78 meter) long and high. The Ark was transported with the help of two bars placed for carrying it, since touching it was forbidden. Anyone who touched it would be struck down by God's wrath. Yahweh ordered that the Tablets of the Law with the Ten Commandments be placed inside the Ark, along with a bowl

of manna, the victuals that had nourished the people of Israel while they were in the desert. After a long journey, the Ark was set up in the Holy of Holies, inside the Temple in Jerusalem. Most likely, the invading troops destroyed the Ark and melted down the gold to produce their own sacred objects, which was a common custom at the time.

UNCERTAIN ROADS
The Biblical texts make no further mention of the Ark after the time of Nebuchadnezzar, though tradition left the door open for hope. The Bible also claims that Jeremiah had time to hide the Ark on Mount Nebo (in Jordan), where it remains hidden. Others looked for it underneath the ruins of the Temple of Solomon. The leading candidate as the Ark's place of rest is Ethiopia, where all the churches contain a replica of the Ark. The English researcher Graham Hancock

argues for this course. The Ark would have been stolen from the Temple by Menelik I (son of King Solomon and the legendary Queen of Sheba, and the future King of Ethiopia), who would have left a copy in its place. Kept for a time on Elephantine Island, in the Nile, it was soon transferred to another island, in Lake Tana, Ethiopia. 800 years later, the Ark would have been carried to Axum (the holiest city in the country), where it is believed that it remains until this day, in the Church of Our Lady Mary of Zion (of the Ethiopian Coptic denomination, within orthodox Christianity). The Ark is under the supervision of a priest, who is the only person authorized to see it. In academic circles, however, it is considered that Menelik is merely a literary character, and that the related story involving the Ark is a medieval invention that originated in the fourteenth century.

The Jews of black Africa

The Lemba people are an African ethnic group that live in South Africa, Zimbabwe, Malawi, and Mozambique. They maintain customs of Semitic origin: they are monotheistic, they dedicate a weekly holy day to their God, who they call Nwali, and they do not eat pork. Diverse genetic studies seem to confirm their relation to the Israelite tribe of the Levites. Their ancestors could have had connections to the *Holy of Holies*. But they are not the only Jewish group in Africa. The Beta Israel people, also known as Falasha ("foreign"), settled in Ethiopia from the Yemen. In 1975 they were included in the Law of Return, which allows them legal emigration to Israel. In 1984, Israel organized Operation Moses toward their "repatriation." In 1991, after the outbreak of civil war in Ethiopia, Israel mounted another blitz operation: in 36 hours, they brought more than 14,000 Falasha to Israel.

IMMIGRANTS
Most Ethiopian Jews (Beta Israel, "House of Israel") today live in Israel. They number around 100,000.

ARTISTIC REPLICA
A careful reproduction of the Ark of the Covenant in a room of the George Washington Masonic National Memorial, in Virginia (United States).

The Ark of the Covenant

The shape and measurements of the Ark are described in Exodus, although not in great detail. The Ark was at the head of the march of the Jewish people in their 40 years of exile, until arriving in Palestine. It was also carried into battle, and its power, according to the Bible, was such that it could decimate enemy armies with its very presence.

REVERENTIAL ATTITUDE
During transport, the Ark was wrapped in a blue cloth. It remained hidden even to those who carried it. They also could not touch it, so bars were used to move it.

LEADING THE PEOPLE
The Ark led the march of the people and the army, and its passage was announced by the sound of the ritual horn (*shofar*).

Sheltered in a church

The Chapel of the Tablet (left), is adjacent to Our Lady of Zion Church in Axum, Ethiopia (pertaining to the Coptic Orthodox Church). Ethiopian tradition states that the Ark of the Covenant is sheltered inside. Only men are permitted access to the chapel, and only a priest can view the Ark. This prevents confirmation of the veracity of the Coptic Church's claim.

SACRED JEWELS
It was coated in gold and had two cherubim on the upper part. Their form is unknown: they may have had animal forms. In addition to the Ten Commandments, the Ark sheltered the budded staff of Aaron and a jar of manna.

Alternative Hypotheses

Did Leonardo da Vinci fabricate the Holy Shroud?

Some defenders of the proto-photography theory (see next page) put forth that it was fabricated by Leonardo da Vinci. Some studies suggest that only the greatest genius of his time could have produced such a work. Leonardo would have used a camera obscura (which, while not producing a perfect image, would provoke the mild deformations of the image printed on the linen) and a special chemical mixture that only he would know and that would be permanently lost with his death in 1519. It is even argued that the human figure on the Shroud is a self portrait. The American artist Lillian Schwartz, famous for postulating in the 1980s that the features on the *Mona Lisa* are perfectly aligned with a self portrait of Leonardo, conducted a similar test to show that another self portrait of the Florentine artist fits perfectly with the features printed on the Holy Shroud. She made her results public in a British television documentary that appeared in June of 2009, *The Da Vinci Shroud*. Since da Vinci was born in 1452, and the existence of the Holy Shroud has been documented since 1355 in Lirey, his work would have been an improved forgery, made by order of the Pope, to replace another earlier forgery. The purpose of the papal order would have been to promote popular devotion during an especially turbulent time (the 14th to 15th centuries) for the Catholic Church.

FORGER
Anonymous portrait by Leonardo da Vinci. Some researchers believe he was the real creator of the image visible on the Shroud of Turin.

Is the Grail in America?

Among the possible places where the Holy Grail would be hidden, one unexpected place has recently been proposed: the American continent. A documentary appropriately entitled *Holy Grail in America* proposes this hypothesis, based on a stone engraved with runic characters found in 1898 in western Minnesota. Apparently the stone bore a series of inscriptions that referred to 8 Goths and 22 Norwegians who made a voyage to the West, where after 14 days they were able to arrive safely, and noted the date of their trip as the year 1362. This message led documentarians Andy and Maria Awes to assume that some Knights Templar could have traveled to America on that date, carrying the treasures in their custody, a journey that was impossible decades earlier. At the other end of the Americas, in Argentina, a group called Delphos, who are self-proclaimed Templars, assert that the Order had founded three cities a century before Columbus arrived in America. These cities had been built in the following locations: one in the province of Chubut, the other in the San Matias Gulf, both in Argentina, and the third in the city of Osorno in Chile.

Is the Holy Shroud a proto-photograph?

In 1993, South African Nicholas Allen, Professor of Fine Arts at the University of Port Elizabeth, stated his theory that the Holy Shroud was a rudimentary photograph. According to his argument, the technology of the period would have allowed this proto-photography to take place. Allen performed numerous experiments, which produced images similar to the Shroud of Turin, in particular with respect to the quality that causes the negative to be a more defined image than the positive. The results of his labors were published in his book *The Turin Shroud and the Crystal Lens,* in 1998. An English researcher, Keith Prince, again tested the theory: he saturated a linen canvas with an emulsion composed of egg white and chrome salt solution, and mounted it on a frame that he placed inside a camera obscura. He opened a small orifice in the opposing wall and exposed a plaster bust in the next room for several hours. Next he washed the canvas and exposed it to heat. The egg white contained in the mixture burned the cloth, but a new wash to remove the egg and leave only the stains made by the heat provided results similar to those found on the Holy Shroud. Barrie M. Schwortz, official documentary photographer of the Shroud of Turin Research Project (STURP) disqualified Allen's thesis in an article in 2000, indicating that "just because the materials exist for these highly advanced technologies does not mean that someone has really created them."

Is the radio-carbon dating wrong?

Sindonologists raise doubt as to whether the fragments analyzed were uncontaminated, since they were extracted from one of the sections of the Shroud that was affected by a fire in 1532. Ash contamination on the cloth could have caused variation in the carbon 14 content in the sample and, consequently, its dating. Most scholars deny that the fire could have modified the properties of the cloth, in addition to emphasizing the cleaning process of the samples. However, others think that the fragments were taken from patches. The chemist Raymond Rogers said he had unused portions of the cloth used as a sample. After analyzing them, he confirmed that the cloth did not come from the original shroud.

CONTAMINATED?
One of the Shroud samples sent to laboratories charged with performing Carbon 14 tests.

Is the Grail incorporeal?

This thesis was advanced by traditionalist writers such as the Frenchman Rene Guenon and the Italian Julius Evola. The different adventures experienced by the heroes of legend symbolize the purification of the soul, until one achieves union with the Grail. The knight Galahad says: "I contemplate here the origin of the great audacities and the cause of the achievements." For Rene Guenon, the Grail possesses an initiatory ("esoteric") symbolism of the most elevated spiritual understanding. It is the "food of immortality" and the "sense of eternity," that provide a mystic experience of the reality that conceals the changing physical world. "Under any exterior form with which it is reviewed," affirms Guenon, "it is always and definitively an expression or a manifestation of the Divine Word." From this perspective, the symbolism of the cup is linked to the heart, which represents at once the center and the spirit. Julius Evola, who in 1934 published *The Mystery of the Grail*, identified the myth of the Grail as an allegory of the knight's initiation, while also emphasizing the spiritual value of the symbolism present in the Arthurian narratives (and in others of pagan origin, such as the Celtic legends), which follow the Grail tradition.

Is the Ark of the Covenant in America?

This hypothesis is picked up by Oscar Vallet in his book *The Ark of the Covenant* (2008), where he clarifies that the explanation is far from being scientific. In the book, the disappearance of the Ark is connected to the Mormons. According to the author, the Ark was brought to North America by the patriarch Lehi, a character cited in the Book of Mormon. He had traveled in the year 600 BCE with the Ark, which was buried in a secret location. Where? The key would be in the very name of Lehi, who appears on page 435 of the Old Testament; this number corresponds to the telephone area code of Utah, where apparently there is a greater proportion of Mormons than in any other area code in the United States. In Utah, there is a mountain called Nebo (the same name as that mountain from which Moses looked upon the Promised Land). The Ark of the Covenant would be hidden precisely at that location.

CELTIC CHALICE
The famous chalice of Ardagh (Ireland), from the thirteenth century. The Celtic influence is evident in the experiences of the Knights of the Round Table in which the Grail appears.

Is the Grail really the descendant of Jesus?

There are those who assert that the Holy Grail is the secret lineage of Christ, literally, the s*ang real* ("royal blood"). This thesis is developed in the successful 1982 book *Holy Blood, Holy Grail*, written by Michael Baigent, Richard Leight, and Henry Lincoln. According to this theory, popularized in the best seller *The Da Vinci Code*, by Dan Brown, Jesus did not die on the Cross, but rather lived and married Mary Magdalene. She conceived a son with him and fled, pregnant, to Languedoc (France). There she gave birth to the descendant of the Messiah, beginning a lineage that continued, hidden, until today. In the sixth century, the dynasty of the Merovingians, members of a tribe of German origin and the first monarchs of France, claimed to be the legitimate heirs of that blood, which forged the concept of kings "by the grace of God." In the mid-twentieth century, the Priory of Scion, a secret society created by the Frenchman Pierre Plantard, claimed rights to the French throne, stating that they were descendants of the Merovingian lineage, although later it was shown that his claims were fraudulently based.

Is it possible that Jesus is not the face on the Holy Shroud?

Another hypothesis that came out in this century appeared in the book *The Second Messiah: Templars, the Turin Shroud, and the Great Secret of Freemasonry*, by Christopher Knight and Robert Lomas. It sustains that Jacques de Molay, the Grand Master of the Order of the Templars, was not burned alive, as history records, but rather was crucified and is the person we can see on the Holy Shroud. The possibility is remote, because, among other reasons, crucifixion was discarded as a method of execution by the Christians, precisely because it was how Jesus had been killed. Another hypothesis proposed that the image of the Grand Master was left deliberately on the cloth, as a secret revenge against the Church, which struck down the Templar order. The record of events does not contradict this hypothesis. Jacques Molay died in a bonfire in 1314, and the Shroud appeared publicly in 1355.

Is the Ark of the Covenant in a Swiss bank?

One of the most adept hypotheses about the whereabouts of the Ark of the Covenant places it in Ethiopia, where it is an important part of the Coptic liturgy, the State religion for many years. In 1974, the emperor Haile Selassie, presumably a direct descendant of King Solomon and the Queen of Sheba, was ousted by a communist revolution. Some years later, due to political instability, Selassie had decided to secretly transfer the Ark to a secure location: a safety deposit box in an undetermined Swiss bank. Haile Selassie was assassinated in 1975, when he was arrested in Ethiopia, and none of his descendants have ever claimed the Ark.

GUARDIAN OF THE ARK
Considered a descendant of Solomon, and head of the Ethiopian Orthodox Church, Haile Selassie (right) assumed care of the Ark that, based on local tradition, is in Ethiopia.

To See and Visit

▼ **OTHER PLACES OF INTEREST**

JERUSALEM
ISRAEL

Holy city of the monotheist, this is the place where Jesus lived His last years. The Church of the Holy Sepulchre is found in the place traditionally identified as Calvary (or Golgotha), where Jesus was crucified. It houses, according to tradition, the sepulchre where Jesus was buried. The Cenacle, where the Last Supper took place, is located on Mount Zion.

OVIEDO
SPAIN

The Cathedral of San Salvador holds within its walls the Holy Shroud of Oviedo, a cloth that, according to tradition, covered the face of Jesus before His burial. It is found in a chapel built specifically for the shroud in the year 840. It has blood stains, although there is no image on the cloth.

VALENCIA
SPAIN

The cathedral of Valencia has housed, since the mid-fifteenth century, a Holy Chalice considered by many to be the one used by Jesus at the Last Supper. It was the official chalice of many popes, and both John Paul II and Benedict XVI used it for mass on their visits to the cathedral.

SCHATZKAMMER
VIENNA, AUSTRIA

A magnificent collection of jewels from the Holy Roman Empire are sheltered here, in addition to the Holy Lance, a fragment of the Cross, and a chalice that has been believed to be the Holy Grail.

The City of Turin

THE CATHEDRAL

The Renaissance cathedral of San Juan Bautista is, since 1578, the place where the Shroud of Turin is housed. The relic is found inside the chapel of the Holy Shroud. The Turin cathedral is one of the most significant pilgrimage sites of the Catholic Church, especially during exhibitions, which are sporadic and irregular. During the five week showing in 1978, some three and a half million people visited the cathedral.

THE CHAPEL

Built at the end of the seventeenth century in the Baroque style by Guarino Guarini, the chapel of the Holy Shroud (in Italian, Cappella della Sacra Sindone or Cappella del Guarini) has a beautiful cupola. The Holy Shroud is normally kept in an urn in which the shroud is found in a horizontal position and covered. During exhibitions, however, it is shown in another urn that is movable, which allows it to be placed in both a vertical and a horizontal position.

OTHER ATTRACTIONS

Located in the Piedmont region in northeastern Italy, the city of Turin is surrounded by the Alps (to the north and west) and is famous for its rich culture and strong industry. It has top-notch museums, such as the Egyptian Museum (the second most important in the world). Not be missed is the Mole Antonelliana, which houses the National Cinema Museum, the Royal Palace, and the Sabauda Gallery, all in the same building as the Egyptian Museum.

Rome, Heart of Catholicism

With the exception of the Vatican, the most important Catholic treasures in the world are found in Rome. The main buildings in which relics related to Jesus Christ are collected are the Basilica of the Holy Cross in Jerusalem and the Archbasilica of Saint John Lateran (photo). Other basilicas in the city, such as San Paolo Extramuros, are located inside Rome but are considered extraterritorial property of the Vatican.

LANGUEDOC
FRANCE

This historical region of France, the capital of which was Toulouse, was the center of the Cathar movement, whose followers were excommunicated and massacred in the Albigensian Crusade at the beginning of the thirteenth century. Some of the castles are considered to be holding places of the Holy Grail and the Ark of the Covenant.

SAINT PETER'S BASILICA
THE VATICAN

Situated within the city of Rome, its main monuments shelter numerous relics of great importance. Saint Peter's Basilica has the most Christian objects (fragments of the Cross, the Holy Lance, and the Veil of Veronica, among others), as well as other relics pertaining to Christian saints from different periods.

GENOA
ITALY

This city holds two very important relics: the Sacro Catino (Holy Chalice), which is found in the Treasury Museum of the cathedral of Genoa; and the Holy Face of Genoa (which many identify with the Mandylion), which is found in the church of Saint Bartholomew of the Armenians.

TORKAPI PALACE
ISTANBUL, TURKEY

The ancient capital of the Ottoman and Eastern Roman Empire, in addition to housing the most sacred relics of Islam, possesses as notable objects the staff of Moses and the turban of Joseph.

Glossary

AMPHORA A tall ancient Greek or Roman jar with a narrow neck and two handles.

ARMISTICE An agreement between two opposing sides in a war to suspend fighting, a truce.

ASCETIC Characterized by the practice of severe self-discipline and abstention, usually for religious reasons.

ASTUTE Showing an ability to accurately assess situations or people.

BEDOUIN Arabic-speaking nomadic peoples of the Middle Eastern deserts.

BIFURCATED Divided into two branches or forks.

CANONICAL Included in the list of sacred books officially accepted as genuine.

CELIBACY The state of abstaining from marriage and sexual relations.

CHERUBIM Angelic beings involved in the worship and praise of God.

CODICES Ancient manuscript texts in book form, plural of codex.

CORPORAL Relating to the human body.

CORRODED Destroyed or damaged slowly by chemical action.

DIASPORA A scattered population whose origin lies within a smaller geographic locale or homeland.

ENIGMA Something that is mysterious or difficult to understand.

EPITAPH An inscription on or at a tomb or grave in memory of the person buried there.

ESCHATOLOGICAL A part of theology concerned with the final events of history or the ultimate destiny of humanity, such as the "end time."

ESOTERIC Intended for or likely to be understood by a small number of people with specialized knowledge.

ETHNARCH Political leadership over a common ethnic group or homogenous kingdom.

EXEGESIS Critical explanation or interpretation of a text, especially scriptural.

FRENETIC Fast and energetic in an uncontrolled way.

GNOMON The part of a sundial that casts a shadow.

HERETIC A person holding an opinion or belief that is at odds with what is generally accepted, especially in religion.

HERMETIC A complete and airtight seal.

INCORPOREAL Having no material existence, not made of matter.

MONOTHEISM A belief that there is only one God.

NASCENT Just coming into existence and showing signs of future potential.

OCCULTISM The belief in or study of supernatural powers.

PAGANISM A religion other than one of the main world religions, especially involving nature worship.

PALYNOLOGY The study of pollen grains and other spores, especially in archaeology.

PENSION A regular payment paid to a royal favorite.

PHILOLOGY The study of language in written historical sources.

RESTITUTION Recompense for injury or loss.

RUNIC Consisting of or set down in characters of certain ancient alphabets (runes).

SANCTIFIED Set apart or declared as holy, consecrated.

SEPULCHER A small room or monument of rock or stone in which a dead person is laid.

TALISMAN An object believed to contain certain magical qualities.

THEOCRATIC Related to a political system in which priests rule and derive their authority from God or gods.

VICTUAL Food or provision intended for consumption.

Further Reading

Barber, Richard. *The Holy Grail: Imagination and Belief.* Cambridge, MA: Harvard University Press, 2004.

Collins, John J. *The Dead Sea Scrolls: A Biography* (Lives of Great Religious Books). Princeton, NJ: Princeton University Press, 2013.

de Wesselow, Thomas. *The Sign: The Shroud of Turin and the Secret of the Resurrection.* New York, NY: Dutton Press, 2012.

Nicolotti, Andrea. Trans. *Hiara Olivera. From the Mandylion of Edessa to the Shroud of Turin: The Metamorphosis and Manipulation of Legend.* Leiden, NL: Brill, 2014.

Parfitt, Tudor. *The Lost Ark of the Covenant: Solving the 2,500 Year Old Mystery of the Fabled Biblical Ark.* New York, NY: HarperCollins, 2009.

Schiffman, Lawrence H. , and James Vanderkam, eds. *Encyclopedia of the Dead Sea Scrolls.* Oxford, UK: Oxford University Press, 2000.

Stefon, Matt, ed. *Christianity* (The Britannica Guide to Religion). New York, NY: Britannica Educational Publishing with Rosen Educational Services, 2012.

Vermes, Geza, ed. *The Complete Dead Sea Scrolls in English.* London, UK: Penguin Classics, 2004.

WEBSITES

Ancient Jewish History: The Ark of the Covenant

http://www.jewishvirtuallibrary.org/the-ark-of-the-convenant

The Jewish Virtual Library presents a detailed account of the scriptural basis of the Ark of the Covenant

Scrolls from the Dead Sea

http://www.loc.gov/exhibits/scrolls/

An online exhibit from the Library of Congress on the Dead Sea Scrolls, with images, contextual information, and material details of artifacts, along with a historical overview of the Scrolls.

The Holy Grail

http://d.lib.rochester.edu/camelot/theme/holy-grail

This page from the Camelot Project at the University of Rochester features an archive of
texts and images related to the legend of the Holy Grail.

The Orion Virtual Qumran Tour

http://virtualqumran.huji.ac.il

The Hebrew University of Jerusalem offers a virtual tour of the Caves of Qumran, providing photo galleries, videos, and background on the archaeological sites.

Index